Pathways of the Heart

Diane Yates

W & B Publishers
USA

Pathways of the Heart © 2015 by Diane Yates

W & B Publishers

For information:
W & B Publishers
9001 Ridge Hill Street
Kernersville, NC 27284
www.a-argusbooks.com

ISBN: 9781635540246

While the author has tried to recreate events, locales and conversations from her memories as well as other eye-witnesses, some events have been fictionalized to help with continuity and flow of the story. In order to maintain their anonymity in some instances. She has changed the names, identifying characteristics, and details of some individuals and places. The people named and still alive have given their permission to use their names in the story.

Cover design by: Ray Polizzi
Printed in the United States of America

Dedication

This book is dedicated to Wallace, Audrey, Linda, Buck, LouAnn, Larry, and to the memory of our beloved mother, Clella.

Acknowledgements

I would like to first thank God for the redemption He gives the world through the blood of Jesus Christ. Without Him I am nothing. I also thank Him for giving me my wonderful husband whose boundless love and support are a constant encouragement to me. My children's belief and trust in me to write a story about their grandmother they loved so much kept me motivated.

I thank my siblings and other family members for their inspiration, pictures, and added insight into the amazing life story of my mother.

Without all of my friends who read the manuscript and offered their encouragement, I wouldn't have been able to persevere through the rejection letters and disappointments.

A special thank you to my agent, Jeanie Loiacono, for praising God and following Him in her tireless efforts to see Pathways of the Heart succeed.

My heart overflows from all the people God has placed in my life. Thank you all.

Chapter One

There is a way that seems right to a man,
but in the end it leads to death.
...Proverbs 16:25

February 20, 1954

The sun brightened an otherwise particularly cold February day in Hartville, Missouri. Inside the two-story brick building at the corner of Main Street and Rolla, Clella sat on the edge of the doctor's table staring blankly at the medical diploma on the wall. She wrung her hands without realizing it. She certainly hadn't anticipated this disturbing outcome.

"But, you could be wrong, right?" She pleaded with the plump, gray-haired man who wore spectacles and perched himself on the stool in front of her. Her voice cracked and tears formed as he confirmed what she feared most.

"No, I'm positive," Doc Mott said again. "You've been pregnant six times before, Clella. I'd think you'd know yourself by now." He patted her arm, then pried the stethoscope from around his neck and laid it on the table. "I'll see you again next month," he added before leaving the room.

Doc Mott wasn't one to gossip or listen to those who did, and therefore, he couldn't have possibly gauged the extent of Clella's distress at this news. When she stood up, she almost collapsed. What was she going to do? Her heart beat wildly. She was stunned, suspended somewhere between yesterday and a very different tomorrow.

When she left his office and stepped onto the sidewalk, she didn't see the children playing hopscotch as she slowly walked past them. She even stepped on the stone one of them threw on the number six square. In her mind, she believed God was punishing her.

Clella thought about Proverbs 31:10 of the Bible, "Who can find a virtuous woman, for her price is far above rubies." Isn't that what she'd always been? She had always intended to be as close to that description as possible: the ever-loving, ever-sacrificing, stand-by-your-man kind of woman; the up-all-hours-of-the-night-with-sick-children, rising-before-daybreak-to-do-the-milking, working-in-the-fields-in-the-afternoon, and spreading-the-table-with-a-feast-by-nightfall kind of woman. Her children "call her blessed" and her husband had "no need of spoil."

God had blessed her with six beautiful children, three boys and three girls. Now, after learning she was having another, she realized this child, this seventh child, complicated her life in a way she never expected.

***

Therefore, shall a man leave his father and mother,
and shall cleave unto his wife: and they shall be one flesh.
.....Genesis 2:24

April, 1954

Inside the massive courtroom of cherry wood and mahogany crown moldings, Clella sat dazed. She heard in the recesses of her mind a voice echoing from a memory long ago, *"Do you, Clella Garner, take Kenneth Lathrom to be your lawfully-wedded husband, to have and to hold from this day forward, for richer or for poorer, for better or for worse, in sickness and in health, until death do you part?"* In that weightless moment, Clella's thoughts drifted in and out of the little country church on that day of beginnings— that day of hope. She thought of the family and friends that had gathered, the flowers, and the eyes of the man who promised to love her and forsake all others— forever. How many times back then had she found acceptance, love, and refuge in his eyes?

Clella jumped back to the present as the gavel hit, wood striking wood. The judge stood, turned, and walked through the door of his chambers. It was over. Their respective attorneys placed their papers into their briefcases almost simultaneously and exited.

In 1954, in the heartland of America where families prayed together and stayed together and divorce was practically non-existent, this judge, with one swift motion, pronounced the marriage between Kenneth and Clella Lathrom dissolved. In a state of shock, Clella turned and stopped face-to-face with Kenneth, his eyes brimming with tears that would surely spill down his face. She couldn't bear that. Quickly, she pushed through the swinging gate ahead of him. She had no choice but to hold her head high regardless of whom she saw in that courtroom. She forged on through the door, down the hall, and out the glass door onto the steps of the Wright County Courthouse. A light breeze brushed her hair and bluebirds twittered in the grass and trees, but she quickened her pace.

She heard the door behind her as she descended the stairs. She didn't turn around, but she knew the steps belonged to Kenneth. She heard him closing the distance between them. Then, from the other side of the middle rail, he grabbed her hand and stopped her. His hand trembled and his voice broke slightly.

"Okay, let's end this madness," he pleaded. Even though his mouth curved up at the corner in that familiar smile and his eyes twinkled that familiar charm, she heard the desperation in his voice. "Let's turn around and go back in there and get married again." His hand tugged tighter on hers, "What do ya say?"

For a moment, she thought her heart stopped beating. Clella looked down at his hand holding hers. His thumb rested on the gold band she still wore on her ring finger.

He noticed also and grasped her hand more firmly. "Clella, come on, let's start all over again."

If only it was that easy. She fought back the tears and pulled her hand free. "I'm afraid not, Kenneth. Not this time." She ran down the stairs and across the parking lot to the '53 green pickup. Luckily, no pedestrians walked in the way, because she didn't look before backing up and speeding down the road.

Highway 38 out of Hartville quickly gave way to rolling hills, streams, red barns, and farmhouses. All those living there were her neighbors and witnesses to the forty-one years of her life, a life she must now leave. Who was to blame? Herself? Kenneth? She didn't know anymore.

Kenneth got the farm and the car; she got their brand-new pickup. Their four children still at home would stay at home. The two oldest, Wallace and Audrey, both grown and living their own lives, wouldn't talk to her. Perhaps they never would.

Kenneth had said, "Why don't we start over?" That's exactly what they must do now, just not together.

The April sun that just this morning shone brightly over blades of green grass, budding tulips, and cherry trees laden with blossoms, now gave way to clouds and rain as Clella turned on the windshield wipers. They would clear the water from the windshield, but nothing could clear the tears flooding her eyes. Events of the past few months played over and over again in her mind as she tried to make sense of them. After crossing the Whetstone Creek Bridge, she pulled over and stopped. Her head fell against the steering wheel as she sobbed uncontrollably.

***

O Lord, the God who saves me, day and
night I cry out before you.
May my prayer come before you; turn your
ear to my cry.
For my soul is full of trouble and my life
draws near the grave.
......Psalms 88:1-3

Kenneth went weak in the knees as he stood on the courthouse steps and watched her drive away. He felt as though someone knocked the breath right out of him. What was he going to do now? The world seemed to have stopped. Forcing each foot in front of the other, he descended the stairs.

"Hi, Kenny," said Ivy Jenkins as she and Opal Smith both passed by, smiling.

Kenneth didn't smile back. He didn't tip his hat or even utter his usual, "How do." In fact, he didn't even appear to notice them. He moved mechanically toward his car, opened the door, and climbed in. Then, he just sat there.

What was he going to do now? The only woman he had ever loved just drove away. He had four kids at home. How could he face them?

An all-too-familiar pain burned in his stomach and chest as he coughed. This pain had plagued him for the past two years or more, but it didn't compare to the present ache in his heart.

Kenneth finally started the car and headed for home. On the way, he pulled a whiskey bottle out of the glove box and drank freely. It scorched as it went down.

He thought about the kids, their kids—now his kids. The oldest, Wallace, served in the Korean War and now lived in Illinois. He was proud of him. Had he told him? Surely he had. Next was Audrey; little Audrey had her own life to deal with—a husband, a job, and two little boys. She, too, lived in Illinois. That left Linda, Buck, LouAnn, and Larry, all waiting for him in Mountain Grove.

Linda was always the apple of his eye and such a pretty thing at the age of sixteen. He'd have to keep his eye on her. Thirteen-year-old Buck, probably the most mischievous child Kenneth had ever seen, used his outgoing charm and personality to trick almost everyone into thinking him a complete angel! LouAnn was only ten. She could, at times, be so brave and yet she was so fragile. She would miss her mother. He started to cry. The youngest, Larry, was only seven. He had struggled with asthma since birth, but Clella always took care of him.

The world weighed heavy on Kenneth. In a split second, he recognized the enormous responsibility the woman bears in raising children. Minutes ago, he felt numb, but now, his emotions came crashing back. Sorrow gave way to anger. How could Clella do this? Anger quickly became fear. He never felt so alone. What was he going to do? Fear subsided into guilt. Kenneth knew that if truth be told, he was the one to blame. If only he could fix it. But no, life would never be the same.

Chapter Two

The Lord God said, "It is not good for man to be alone. I will make a helper suitable for him."
......Genesis 2:18

August 1928

One wouldn't call the Garner home ritzy, but for Competition, Missouri in the Ozarks, the two-story Victorian-style might well have been a mansion. In one of the upstairs bedrooms, fifteen-year-old Clella studied her petite figure in the mirror while butterflies danced in her stomach. Why should being baptized in the creek today after this morning's church service make her so nervous? Her fingers trembled as she ran the brush through her hair. The door flew open and her older sister, Essa, ran in to retrieve the Bible from the nightstand.

"Hurry, Clellie, we're about to leave," she said before dashing back out.

All the names of the Garner girls ended in "a", but they pronounced them as if they ended in "ie". The only exceptions to this rule were the youngest, Mag, whose name was actually Verla, but they all called her Mag, and most times, family and friends pronounced Clella's name with an "a" at the end.

Clella heard twelve-year-old Mag bounding down the stairs, the loud crashing steps drowning out the argument below between her other sister, Delphie, and her mom. She could only make out the deep rumble of her father's voice when the arguing stopped completely. That would be her father's stern words. John Wesley Garner ruled his household with a firm hand, yet not without love.

Everybody called him Judge, probably because he was one. Clella not only loved her father, but also respected and admired him. Certainly, when he spoke, everybody listened.

Hettie Garner, their mild-mannered, hard-working, and devoted mother, was raising the last of her children on their rich farmland. Her exceptional ability as seamstress and cook never failed to provide clothing and food for those she loved. She sewed all her family's garments and spent endless hours canning and preserving the bounties of their harvest. Their cellar was always full. She taught her girls how to be ladies with tenderness. Clella couldn't remember a time when her mother hadn't been there for her.

The Garner household wasn't that much different from others in Wright County in 1928. Clella was one of ten children, next to the youngest. With five of them either married, away at school, or living on their own, that left only four girls at home: Essie, Delphie, Clella, and Mag.

Well, there had been another little girl—her parents' third child. As with so many families in that era, little Ethel died from a fever at fourteen months of age. Even though Clella hadn't been born yet, she knew the story well. Her sister's death always haunted her father, who was away working in Oregon at the time.

Hettie sent word to him of little Ethel's illness, but news traveled slowly and didn't reach him for several days. Meanwhile at home, Ethel's temperature kept climbing despite her mother's nursing efforts. Even sponge bathing had no effect. It had been clear the child's fate lay in God's hands.

Though he knew nothing of her illness at the time, John later said that the night she died he had an awful dream in which he walked forever through the desert, carrying his toddler in his arms, frantically searching for water for her.

"The Lord giveth and the Lord taketh away," her mother always said, or "the Lord knows best," or "God works in mysterious ways." Her family wasn't all that religious, but her parents taught her to believe in God and His awesome power (even if she didn't always understand it).

Today, Clella would be baptized because of a decision she made on a Sunday not too long ago. She sat in the third pew when God spoke to her about the sin in her life. She always prided herself on being good and doing what she was told, but that day the preacher said, "Everyone sins, and that sin separates you from God, because God can have no part with sin." Suddenly, Clella knew her so called "being good" was just as sinful as filthy rags.

The pastor preached on, "Adam first sinned in the garden of Eden, and God had told him if he and Eve ate of that tree, they would surely die. So death and separation from God became the punishment for Adam's disobedience. All men have sinned and, therefore, face the same punishment. But Jesus came and never sinned so that he could die in our place." Then the preacher beckoned, "Come and wash away your sins with the blood of the Savior." Up until that moment, Clella never understood why Jesus died on the cross. She practically ran all the way to the altar, tears streaking down her face. That very instant, her heart and life were changed.

Now, this morning, when the service was over, the congregation would all go to the creek where she would follow the Lord in baptism. She wondered who all might be there. She hoped to see Jacob Harvey, a really nice young man who had been paying her a lot of attention lately. Another stroke of the brush and she tied a ribbon in her hair.

When Essie mentioned something yesterday at the supper table about Kenneth Lathrom coming, Clella dropped her fork in the middle of her plate. Kenneth was the one person she didn't care if she saw or not. He had been a thorn in her side since childhood. He always seemed intent on teasing and tormenting her. Lately, she heard tales of his developed tastes for local moonshine. Just last week, the feds had seized the Bettis farm and had thrown Otis and Clive Bettis in jail after finding the trap door to their homemade distillery. Why, even last month, authorities shot and killed a man in Ava while he tried to smuggle the devil drink up north.

Clella couldn't deny the fact Kenneth had grown into a good-looking young man, tall, slender, but sturdy, with dark features and tanned skin. His deep brown eyes seemed to sparkle as the young ladies fell spellbound when he walked past them in town, tipping his hat slightly and offering a "how do." It was enough to turn Clella's stomach.

Besides, unlike Jacob, who was ambitious and dreamed of going places, Kenneth had no goals. Farming was Kenneth's calling. His father was a schoolmaster, but he tended the land.

Clella placed her neatly-folded handkerchief in her purse just before the car horn sounded outside.

"Clellie, will you come on? You're going to make us all late," her mother yelled from the foot of the stairs. "Everyone's already in the car and waiting."

Clella ran down the stairs, sending their calico cat out the screen door and scurrying across the yard. "Sorry, Mom, it's just I can never get my hair to do," Clella said before climbing in the back seat of their automobile. They were one of the few families in Wright County who possessed a gasoline-powered vehicle. However, her father still kept horses and much of their travel relied on them, because of how easily they pulled the sleigh in the winter snow.

It certainly wasn't winter now with the August sun beating down its searing heat. On the way to the little church in the valley, they passed many farms. Some had only log cabins or small shacks for dwellings, and none had inside plumbing. The beautiful rolling hills of Wright County disguised to all except perhaps those who lived there, their difficult life. The ride to church reminded Clella of her family's blessings.

Chapter Three

*Therefore, if anyone is in Christ, he is a new
creation;
the old has gone, the new has come!
......2 Corinthians 5:17*

The old black truck rattled and clanked as it stirred the dust off the dirt road, passing the little white schoolhouse where the road forked. Kenneth barely slowed down, taking a hard right in front of the old Hopkins place. The summer heat penetrating the windshield from the noon-day sun wilted his freshly ironed shirt. Unless that preacher got long winded again, he was going to be late.

Kenneth pushed down on the accelerator, forcing the truck to a greater speed and topping the hill by Uncle Se's place. He looked across the rolling field of alfalfa toward the house to see if Uncle Se's car was parked in its usual spot under the oak tree. No. That meant he must have gone to church this morning, and by now would be down at the water. Good ole Uncle Se. If it hadn't been for him, Kenneth would never have learned about the picnic and Clella's baptism.

"Why don't you come, too?" Uncle Se invited him. "A little preachin' 'ould do ya good. Give ya a chance to get close to Clella."

Clella was about the prettiest girl around these parts, at least to Kenneth. Fact was, he hadn't been able to think about anyone else since the sixth grade when she sat in front of him, writing her assignment on her slate just like his father instructed. His father, the schoolteacher, taught all eight grades in the little one-room school. Kenneth could never get Clella to talk to him, though. One day, he decided to pull her pigtails; surely, she'd get mad and turn around. But not Clella. No, she just leaned forward and pulled her hair in front of her. So he resorted to shooting spit wads.

At first, she ignored them, brushing them away, but the third one did the trick! Clella jumped to her feet, spun around and screamed at him, "Stop that this instant!" Then she turned red in the face, but it was too late. Mr. Lathrom stood beside them both.

"What's going on here, Kenneth?" he demanded of his son. Clella quietly slipped back into her seat.

"I...I...just," he stammered. With his father being stricter than most, Kenneth knew he faced punishment. Mr. Lathrom had a soft spot for Clella. She never did anything wrong in his eyes.

"Clella?" Mr. Lathrom raised his brows. She nervously glanced at the razor strap hanging in the corner before speaking.

"Ah, I'm sorry, Mr. Lathrom," Clella said. "It's my fault. I didn't mean to disturb the class."

Mr. Lathrom studied her for a moment. "Well, you can both stay after school, and I don't want to hear so much as a peep out of either of you again."

Kenneth released the breath he'd been holding and knew Clella just saved him. From that moment on, she held his heart. But in all the four years since then, she still wouldn't pay him any attention.

The dust trail behind the moving vehicle continued down into the valleys and up over the hills. Kenneth ran his tongue over his dry lips to keep them from sticking to his teeth. He reached under the seat for his whiskey bottle.

"What's the matter with you?" he scolded himself. "You can't have whiskey on your breath around all those church folks." He'd just wait until he got to Whetstone Creek. There'd be punch and plenty to eat. He knew everyone was supposed to bring a covered dish, but no one would expect it of him. They all knew the Lathrom kids didn't have a mother, least ways one who could cook. After his mother died, Kenneth's father, De (short for DeSoto), married a pretty woman from back east, but she didn't like to get her hands dirty. Kenneth was lucky he talked his sister, Initia, into ironing his shirt this morning much less preparing a dish for him to take to the baptism and all-day picnic of the Oak Grove Baptist Church.

When the truck topped the hill, he saw the creek flowing across the road below and a couple of cars and buggies parked in a clearing off to the left at the bottom of the hill. He slowed the vehicle down and pulled over with the others.

The sound of the congregation singing drifted over the few parked cars and tethered horses. He winced as he unmistakably detected Minnie Massey singing her usual flat notes here and there. Gosh darn! Why didn't someone teach that girl to sing or tell her to keep quiet?

"Shall we gather at the river, the beautiful, the beautiful river, gather with the saints at the river that flows by the throne of God." **(At The River,** Robert Lowery, 1864)

Kenneth bent over and snipped a weed with his hand and saw Jim Robinett walking toward him. Jim's dad, Jesse, owned a spread on Highway 38, about six miles out of Hartville. Jim was older than Kenneth, but they were good friends. They greeted each other quietly, out of respect for the preacher, who now spoke from where he stood thigh-high in the water. Kenneth stuck the tip of the weed in his mouth, sucking and moving it slightly with his teeth while turning his full attention to Clella, who was waist deep in the water.

"This is my little sister in Christ, Clella Garner," the preacher announced. Facing her, he asked, "Clella, do you know that you're saved? Have you given your heart to Jesus?"

"Yes," she answered, nodding her head.

"Then I baptize you, my little sister, in the name of the Father, Son, and the Holy Ghost, buried in the likeness of His death." Then, with his left arm at her back for support, he raised his right hand to her head and pushed her back, plunging her beneath the water before raising her up again. "Raised in the likeness of His resurrection." The crowd cheered and Clella pushed back the wet brown hair from her face, smiling at the preacher as he clasped her hand in his. "Walk in the newness of life."

Kenneth watched Clella's shapely figure slowly emerge from the water as she waded to the shore. Her wet dress adhered to the natural swells of her bosom, clung to the tiny wisp of her waist, and wrapped around each thigh. She went and stood beside her parents and her sister, Essie.

With her back turned, she never even noticed him! Uncle Se did, though, and tipped his hat in Ken's direction. It looked like it was going to be another day of Clella ignoring him. Maybe he really should put some interest in someone else. Eva Hicks always hung on him. Maybe, he'd go talk to her.

In the shade, back away from the river, sat a table loaded with all kinds of delicious dishes. While lining up for food, Kenneth eyed Clella talking to Jacob Harvey quite a ways in front of him. Jim Robinett followed Ken in line. Jim was tall and fairly good looking, but usually a loner.

"Hey, Kenny, you know about the dance Saturday night, right?" Jim asked.

"Sure. You goin'?"

"I'll be there. I mean Essie and me." Jim's face beamed with pride.

Kenneth turned to look him directly in the eyes. "Naw. You kiddin' me?" Kenneth smiled in amazement. Jim shook his head, but Kenneth continued in disbelief. "Really? Essie? I thought Essie and Echo..."

"No. It's going to be tall, slender Essie Garner with me. What's more, she says Clella'll come, too, if I can find her a decent date." Jim's eye held a gleam in it and he grinned when he added, "I just don't know who I'm going to think of!"

"Hum, that's a tough one!" Kenneth said, rubbing his chin. "Let me think. I guess, to help you out and all, maybe I could volunteer."

"I sort of figured you would."

"You'd better make sure it's okay with Clella first." Kenneth suggested. "She seems to be paying a lot of attention to Harvey up there."

"I told Essie I was going to ask you and she said you'd be good." Jim picked out two pieces of fried chicken before dipping out a heap of baked beans.

"She did?" Ken asked, almost missing the fried chicken. He excused himself and reach over those in line behind him.

"Yep. She even said she thought Clella liked you."

"Are you joshin' me?"

"You know I wouldn't do that."

"All right! It's a date then." Kenneth's elation dissipated when he looked to see Clella and Jacob Harvey, their plates filled with food, sitting down on a quilt in the shade beside some other young people. He fumed at the sight of Jacob sitting next to her and the two of them talking and laughing. He'd gone through all the trouble of getting dressed and coming to this stupid picnic only to watch someone else making time with his girl. Well, she wasn't exactly his girl, but she would be.

Once, Clella glanced in Kenneth's direction and smiled, but it caught him off guard, as if he thought his face might actually reveal his thoughts, so he quickly looked away.

Later, when the sun cast shadows and everyone began gathering their belongings, Kenneth climbed in his truck, started it up, and drove away without having said a word to the beautiful girl who held his heart.

Instead, he reached beneath the seat and retrieved the bottle of moonshine, put it to his lips, and took a big swig. "I wonder what Eva Hicks is doing tonight?" he pondered aloud.

Chapter Four

"I want to go, too," Mag pleaded with her sisters as they all walked down the dirt road in the August heat. "Please."

"You can't go. You're just a baby," Clella reminded her. She took great pleasure in the fact that there was at least one out of nine siblings younger than her.

"I am not. I'm twelve years old and I can dance just as good as either of you."

"Now, Mag," Essie reasoned, "you know Mom and Dad won't let you go." Clella knew Essie, being the oldest of the three, felt it was her duty to bring Mag back down to Earth.

Returning to the original subject, Clella asked Essie, "Are you sure I have to go with Kenneth Lathrom? Couldn't Jim find someone else, like Jacob?"

"What do you have against Kenneth?" Essie asked. "I think he's very nice looking and he's every bit a fine gentleman."

"I don't know. He's ornery." She deliberately kicked a rock with her shoe. "He used to pester me all the time just for meanness. He's never going to amount to anything." She turned and walked backward so she could look at Essie as she talked. "Besides, you didn't see him Sunday at the picnic. I smiled at him, but he didn't even acknowledge me." Clella indeed dreaded attending her first dance with the likes of Kenneth Lathrom.

They heard a truck coming from behind so they all lined up single-file on the narrow country road, maneuvering through the dirt mounds and tall weeds on the side. Suddenly, the horn sounded, AH-OOO-GAH, causing them to jump. As the vehicle swerved right, the girls dove into the weeds to avoid being hit. When the Ford truck passed, the driver turned and looked out the back window. Clella recognized Kenneth Lathrom and quickly stuck her tongue out.

Essie laughed. "I wonder if that's acknowledgement enough!"

He must have turned around because, in a few minutes, the truck returned, and this time, Kenneth stopped and jumped out. He marched right up to Clella.

"Did you stick your tongue out at me?" With pursed lips, he towered above her, dangerously close. Although his boldness shocked her, she wasn't one to be bullied. She stepped even closer and stood as tall as her five feet four inches allowed.

"I most certainly did! How dare you– running us off the road driving like that!"

He stepped back. "Well, you should watch where you're walking and stay out of the way."

Same old Kenneth, Clella thought, but her breath caught in her throat because he sure was handsome. Long hours in the sun had darkened his skin and the dust from the road sprinkled his rich brown hair. He was lean but muscular, no doubt from plowing and splitting rails. Even so, she struggled to ignore him as she brushed the dirt off her clothes.

"You going to the dance with me or not?" he asked.

She looked up into his deep brown eyes, and, for a moment, had the impulse to yell, "I wouldn't go with you if you were the last man on Earth!" but reconsidered and replied, "Yes, I'm going with you."

He blinked before clearing his throat and backing up another step, "Fine, then...I'll...see you...at seven."

She wouldn't have accepted, but Mom and Dad finally gave their permission for her to attend a dance and, even if she had to go with the likes of him, she didn't intend to miss it. Wanting to have the last word, she hollered, "Fine," after he'd already started walking away.

***

"Mom, we're home," Mag yelled the minute the three of them entered the house.

Hettie answered from the sewing room, "Come in here, girls."

Clella took off her hat and joined Essie and Mag. They found their mother sitting at the sewing machine making another dress for one of her girls. Clella knew her mother's endless love and provision for her family was the bonding fiber of their existence. Her father provided the discipline, but Hettie gave her daughters the perfect example of a godly wife and mother.

"Clella, I took this dress of Essie's and cut it down to fit you," she said. "It doesn't fit Essie anymore, and I remembered how much you liked it." Hettie pulled the finished royal blue dress away from the machine and held it up for all the girls to see. She had added a dainty collar and shortened the pleats. "I thought you could wear it to the dance Saturday night."

"Oh, Mom, it'll be perfect!" Excitedly, Clella took the dress and held it up in front of the mirror. What used to be Essie's dress now belonged to Clella. A few changes such as the lace collar, made it just like new.

Mag pulled grapes off the bunch in a bowl and popped them in her mouth one by one, listening. Then she added, "Yeah, but after the way Kenneth Lathrom behaved today, Mom, I don't think you should let her go with him."

Hettie raised her eyebrows curiously. "What happened?"

"Oh, nothing." Clella said, trying to act nonchalant. When her mother wasn't looking, she stuck her tongue out at her younger sister. Sometimes, she could be such a little brat.

"He practically ran us off the road with his dad's truck," Mag continued.

Clella laughed, trying to diffuse any improprieties her mother might conceive. "Oh, he did not."

"She sure wasn't singing his praises out there on the road," Mag persisted. "You should a heard 'em yelling at each other like two old married folks. I was afraid he was gonna hit her or something."

"Mom, Mag's exaggerating again," Essie said, settling the debate.

"No, I'm not." Even though Mag protested, Essie's explanation satisfied Hettie.

"Go wash up now, all of you, and help me cook supper."

**

The dress fit Clella perfectly. The darts in the bodice accentuated her breasts, and the lower waistline moved with her hips as she walked, hinting at the tiny span of her waist hidden beneath. Now, if only she could get her hair to do, as she brushed and shaped and brushed and shaped. She rolled it in rags the night before and reset it today, but it still wasn't holding a curl.

Essie entered the room with a curling iron in hand just as Clella lost all patience. "Here, I just took it off the fire. Sit down, turn around, and let's see what your older sister can do."

Later, as Kenneth opened the back door of Jim's father's Model T, Clella couldn't help but notice how nice he looked in his black pinstriped suit, shined shoes, and crisp, white shirt. For some reason, her stomach tied in knots and her palms started sweating.

Essie and Jim talked with ease in the front seat. Clella looked out the window most of the time, anything to keep from looking at Kenneth. She wished she didn't have to sit this close to him and began regretting her decision to go to the dance at all. He hadn't even told her she looked nice.

"So, have you been run off the road lately?" Ken asked. The gold flecks in his eyes danced teasingly as the corner of his mouth curved slightly.

"No, but then I haven't seen you speeding up and down it either."

"Don't worry. Next time you're walking, I'll see what I can do."

She turned away. "I can believe that," she mumbled under her breath.

Jim asked, "Kenny, what's this I hear about Aubrey leaving?" Aubrey was Kenneth's older brother.

"Yeah, he's going out to Oregon next week. They're working up in the timber. I hear some of those fellas make anywhere from two dollars on up."

"With your dad taking the school in Mansfield, who's going to help you harvest and put in wood for winter?" Jim asked.

"Oh, Eric's getting where he's quite a bit of help."

Clella stole a glance at Kenneth during this conversation and saw for the first time the weathered lines around his eyes. She knew with Mr. Lathrom busy running the school, all the chores rested squarely on Kenneth and Aubrey's shoulders.

Their sister, Initia, did well to cook and clean for them, and Eric was only ten.

They parked the Model T on the square in Mansfield. The fiddler, guitar pickers, and harmonica players filled the air with lively music. Kenneth offered Clella his arm and escorted her to the pavilion. Everyone pretty much knew each other. The two of them stood around talking to various acquaintances while the musicians played one tune after another. Clella began to think Kenneth didn't dance and started looking to see who else might ask her.

When Kenneth went to get them both some punch, Jacob snuck up behind her. "You look stunning in that dress. It's your color," he said slyly.

"Why thank you, Sir." She smiled. Not only did he notice how she looked, but he mentioned it first thing.

"May I have this dance?" He asked. He looked dashing.

"You sure may."

The band played "Whispering." As the two of them moved together to the music, Clella laughed. Then, Jacob pulled her close. Too close. Clella hadn't ever been this close to a man before and she didn't think she liked his forwardness. As their dance ended, she welcomed the release.

"Hey, I've got something I want to show you," he said, grasping her hand and leading her away from everyone.

"I can't leave," she told him, but he wouldn't let go. He led her over behind the bushes where the light didn't shine.

"You look mighty pretty tonight," he whispered, taking her into his arms and boldly claiming her lips with his own. She struggled, pushing away, but he held her fast. She managed to break her mouth away from his disgusting slobber just enough to release a muffled scream. She heard movement approaching them.

Kenneth muttered something as he pulled Jacob from her, then punched him three times, one right after the other. With the first blow to his stomach and the last one square on the nose, he left Jacob flat on his back. "Go on home, Harvey. The night's over for you," he warned.

Silent tears spilled over Clella's cheeks as Kenneth wrapped his arms around her. "Are you okay?" he asked. She nodded. "Did he hurt you?" She shook her head as Kenneth gave her his handkerchief and walked her back.

She trembled beneath his touch. They stopped under a lamppost.

"I'm sorry about that," he apologized. "I've wanted to do that to him ever since that church picnic."

"What?" She wasn't sure she heard correctly.

"Oh, I didn't like the way he sat next to you that day." She nodded as if agreeing, and finished blowing her nose. Their eyes met and they burst out laughing.

"You sure you're okay? You want to go home?" he asked.

"Not me. I feel like I just got here." She didn't understand it, but somehow, she felt rejuvenated.

The sound of "Harvest Moon" played in the background. Finally, Kenneth asked, "Would you like to dance?"

"I thought you didn't dance."

"Who told you that?"

He held out his hand and she grasped it. Her fingers tingled inside the warmth of his. As he walked her to the dance floor, his eyes gleamed. They looked at each other, smiling. Then, he swept her away. How wonderfully he danced. As they moved together, fireflies sprinkled lights here and there, making the moment seem magical.

Later, as they drove home, Clella didn't sit as close to the door. Kenneth slowly reached out and placed his hand over hers. The summer night suddenly got warmer, and the stars in the sky shined a little brighter.

Chapter Five

But He said unto me, "My grace is sufficient
for thee."
.....2 Corinthians 12:9 KJV

A lone candle in the living room lit the otherwise dark house. Clella recognized their mother sitting in the rocking chair waiting up for them.

"Good night, Mama," Essie called out as she climbed the stairs. Clella would have joined her, but stopped. She thought it strange when her mother didn't answer.

"Mama?" She walked closer only to realize her mother was crying.

"Mama, what's wrong?" Clella knelt in front of her. Hettie pulled a handkerchief from her apron pocket and blotted her eyes.

"Oh, nothing, Sweetheart. Did you have a good time?"

Clella would have liked nothing more than to share all the fun she had. She wanted to tell her how wonderful Kenneth was and how exhilarating it was to dance in his arms, but she knew something serious troubled her mother.

"I had a great time, Mama, but please tell me what's wrong."

Hettie started crying again. "It's Artie," she managed, but couldn't say more. Artie, Clella's oldest sister, lived far away in Washington State. Clella imagined the worst. She noticed her mother held a letter in her hand.

"What, Mama? Is she all right?"

Hettie dried her eyes. "I'm afraid not. The doctors don't expect her to live. Seems she has a mysterious illness they don't know how to treat."

"Oh, Mama, no." She hugged her mother while she eyed the picture on the mantle of Artie standing next to her mother. Artie's dress had puffed sleeves. Her hair was softly and meticulously fluffed around her face and formed into a fashionable bun on top. She was the very portrait of beauty and elegance.

"I knew when she left," Hettie cried, "I would never see her again."

Clella asked, "Does Papa know?"

"Yes. He's taking it pretty hard. Spent most of the evening in the barn."

***

Sleep eluded Clella that night. Artie was twenty-two years older and had left to go out west with her husband when Clella was only three. Clella didn't really remember her, but she knew her mother had a close bond with her firstborn. Now, the family might never see her sister again this side of heaven.

Still, her thoughts couldn't help but drift back to Kenneth and the enchanted evening they shared. Kenneth, what a surprise! He could certainly be charming. And laughs—she couldn't remember when she had laughed so much. She hadn't wanted the night to end. She kept remembering him saying he didn't like the way Jacob sat next to her at the picnic. Surely, that meant he had liked her all along. She always thought otherwise because of the relentless way he teased her.

***

The next week passed slowly. The Garner family sent numerous letters of encouragement, prayers, and love to Artie in Washington. How helpless they all felt. They were totally dependent on news of their beloved arriving by mail. Artie didn't write herself. Instead, letters arrived from either her husband or one of the children. All the Garner family could do now was wait, watch, and pray.

Clella didn't hear from Kenneth during that whole week. That night of the dance now seemed like a marvelous dream that she held close to her heart. Other than the strong desire to see him, she had no reason to doubt the good time they had together meant as much to him as it did to her. They had held hands on the way home and stared into each other's eyes. She had fully believed he would pay her a visit before now. That Saturday, she dressed especially nice when the family got ready to go to Hartville to do their weekly shopping. Usually, all the country folks spent extra time at the square, visiting with friends. Surely, Kenneth would be there. She couldn't wait to see him again.

After they arrived, Essie saw Jim, Mag played with friends from school, and Clella talked to different friends throughout the day. She kept a constant eye out for Kenneth, but he never came. As the family drove home, she stared out the window and said not a word. Her heart ached, but the cherished memories of the dance would have to be enough for now.

Two long weeks passed since she last saw him and still he never came calling. On Sunday, the family prepared to go to the Lord's house to worship. As the Garners arrived at their little country church in the valley, they filed one-by-one into their row and sat surrounded by friends. The morning sun already warmed the room, and Clella watched her father take out his handkerchief and gently dry his brow. It reminded her of the handkerchief Kenneth gave her that night so long ago.

Before the service began, Clella looked about the room as Eva Hicks and Ivy Smith sat behind her. Clella overheard Eva talking. When she mentioned Kenneth Lathrom and something about the creek last Friday night, Clella strained to hear every word. Eva and the other girl started giggling. Essie, who sat next to Clella, talked with Jim. Their conversation made it impossible to hear everything Eva said.

Clella turned red, fuming. She clenched her jaw tight, but it didn't prevent the knife stabbing pain in her heart. Kenneth Lathrom— she should have known better! He had betrayed her. Maybe he didn't have feelings for her at all. Maybe he was seeing Eva Hicks and that's why he hadn't come around. Her mind wandered, keeping her from hearing much of the sermon. When it was over, Clella fumed all the way to the car.

That night, her mood still hadn't improved. While getting ready for bed, she pulled her nightgown on with such force, it nearly ripped. When she slammed the dresser drawer shut, Essie sighed.

"What's wrong with you? You've hardly said a word all day!"

Clella glanced at her, pulled the brush through her hair one more time, before slamming it on the vanity. "Did you hear Eva Hicks in church this morning?"

"No. Did she say something to upset you?" Clella intended to relay the story objectively, but couldn't help but hiss and groan between sentences. When she finished, Essie tried to console her. "I wouldn't put any stock in anything Eva Hicks said. Maybe Kenneth's just been busy with the harvest."

Clella threw back the bed covers. "No, if I never see him again, it will be too soon."

"I'll see if Jim can find out anything," Essie offered.

"Don't bother." Clella turned over in bed and pounded her feather pillow a couple of times before resting her head on it. Essie blew out the lamp.

The next two weeks passed and it was Clella's birthday. The family planned a nice dinner. John Garner even invited Jim Robinett to join them. Essie and Jim were seeing a lot of each other. In fact, Jim had been to the house many times. He and Essie played card games with John and Hettie.

"There she is, the birthday girl herself!" her father announced as Clella came down the stairs. "Sweet sixteen today."

The family began to sing "Happy Birthday," and Clella beamed. She saw her mother standing next to her father, then Delphie, Mag, Essie, Jim, and...the smile disappeared and the color left her face. Kenneth Lathrom stood next to Jim. She glanced at the table and quickly counted the place settings. Sure enough, there was one extra. Who had invited him? If Essie invited him and didn't tell her, she'd wring her neck!

She sat at the opposite end of the table and deliberately ignored him. Essie sat next to Clella, and Clella gave her a questioning look. Essie shook her head and shrugged. Judge Garner said grace and Hettie sliced the roast beef.

"So, Clella, what is it you want for your birthday?" asked Jim.

"I really wanted to learn to drive the car, but Dad says no."

Her father laughed. "You can hardly control the power of one horse. How do you expect to control the power of forty horses in that expensive automobile parked outside?"

"I don't think that's very fair," Clella started to argue, but her father interrupted her.

"Now, Clella."

"I can teach her, Sir," Kenneth quickly offered. "I only have my dad's truck, but it's pretty easy to drive."

"No, I wouldn't consider it," she snapped. "Jim, I also wanted..."

"Why not?" Kenneth challenged.

Essie quickly interjected, "She means a truck is probably harder to control than a car."

Clella continued confidently, "No, mostly I'm rather particular about who teaches me."

"What does that mean?" Kenneth's voice rose slightly and everyone stopped talking. All eyes first looked at Kenneth and then at Clella.

"Well," Clella responded calmly while pouring gravy over her mashed potatoes, "I just think the person I choose to teach me should be able to invest enough time to finish what they start." She looked at him and smiled.

He seemed to consider saying something, but glanced around the table at everyone and remained silent.

Hettie served a delicious birthday cake along with homemade ice cream, a very special treat, even for a birthday.

When the family retired to the parlor, Clella slipped away upstairs. She closed the door to her bedroom and leaned against it. She took several deep breaths, trying to calm the racing of her heart. Her birthday had turned into a nightmare. *What is Kenneth Lathrom doing here?* She needed to put an end to this once and for all. She crossed the room to her dresser and opened the drawer. She retrieved what she came for and put it safely in her pocket.

When she returned downstairs, she didn't meet Kenneth's gaze, and successfully ignored him until he said his goodbyes. At the front door, her resolve faltered some as she lingered in the depth of those brown eyes. What did she read in them? Bewilderment? Hurt? It didn't matter. She reached inside her pocket and pulled out his handkerchief, which she had carefully washed, ironed, and neatly folded the day after the dance.

"I believe this belongs to you, Kenneth. Thank you," she said. She purposefully spoke in a cold tone.

He looked puzzled. With his left hand, he tucked it away in his pants pocket, but with his right, he reached into his shirt, next to his heart, and there he retrieved a folded dainty square cloth tied with baby blue ribbon.

"Happy birthday, Clella." He lifted her hand and placed it gently in her palm then clasped both his hands over hers. She swallowed hard and found a beautifully-embroidered linen handkerchief with little pink rosettes and mint green leaves.

"I wanted to give you something, and well, Initia made it for me to give you," he explained.

Clella struggled to find her voice. Unable to lift her eyes to face him, she uttered softly, "Thank you. Please tell her it's beautiful." He slipped out the front door and down the steps.

Chapter Six

A righteous man is cautious in friendship, but
the way of the wicked leads them astray.
......Proverbs 12:26

The next week, Clella wondered why Kenneth distanced himself from her, yet surprised her with his gift. She didn't see him again until church on Sunday. A good crowd packed the house in spite of it being harvest time. Clella, Essie, and Jim sat in the second row. As if guided by fate, she turned around just before the service started to see Kenneth enter. His gaze caught hers. He looked handsome in a pressed white shirt and khaki trousers.

Clella started to step out and ask Kenneth to sit with them when Eva Hicks made her move. She weaseled her way to his side and slipped her hand in the crook of his arm and led him away. He seemed to go willingly, but he glanced again at Clella, who quickly turned around and sat down.

Mrs. Oliver, who played the piano for the congregation, wasn't there this morning, so the preacher asked Clella if she would fill in. Clella didn't really play, having had no formal lessons, but she did know a few songs and loved to play them. After the third song, "The Sweet By and By," Clella took her seat. She didn't hear a word of the sermon. All she could think about was Kenneth Lathrom and how much she hated him. She had half a mind to tell him so, too. In fact, that's what she decided she'd do. Immediately after the service, she would go right up to him and tell him just what she thought of him. She might tell Eva Hicks what she thought of her, too.

"Amen," Brother Cecil closed the service in prayer and all began shuffling out of the little church. With determination, Clella started toward where Kenneth had been sitting with Eva Hicks, but he was nowhere to be seen. She looked to the left, then right, and back behind her.

"Clella, are you all right?" Essie asked.

"What? Oh, I'm fine," she answered, still searching. Finally, she walked outside. John, Hettie, and Mag Garner had already climbed in their car and Delphie stood on the other side. Clella felt the slight nip in the air and noticed the leaves falling from the trees which blushed with autumn colors.

"Jim is going to give me a ride home on his horse," Essie said.

Clella finally spotted Kenneth under the tree untying his chestnut steed. He walked over with the reigns in his hands, tipped his hat, and said, "Morning, Clella. You want to join me and we'll ride alongside Jim and Essie?"

Clella hesitated. She watched as Essie climbed on back with Jim. She looked around, but didn't see Eva Hicks anywhere. Kenneth stood there tall, yet gentle, with eyes piercing hers. Her resolve slowly melted.

"What do ya say?" he asked, looking up at the blue sky. "I don't figure we have many nice days like this one left before winter sets in. Better take advantage of 'em."

"Clella, are you coming?" her mother called from the car.

She looked at her mother, then back at him, trying to decide what to do. "No, I think I'll ride with Kenneth," she answered.

"That's my girl," he muttered in her ear before he mounted his horse. Kenneth seemed sure of himself as he sat in the saddle and helped Clella up.

"Where's the truck?" she asked.

"Dad needed it. Chester'll do fine."

Clella sat in the saddle behind Kenneth. Though she agreed to the ride, her anger still burned. She didn't want to hold onto him and, in fact, the heat from his body being so close to hers was unnerving. Essie laughed at something Jim said, but Clella remained quiet. She refused to forget Kenneth's neglect. They enjoyed one heavenly night of dancing, but then she didn't hear from him again until her birthday, but it seemed he managed to spend time with Eva.

"You okay?" he asked.

"I'm fine."

"You can put your arms around me if you want," he offered.

"I'm all right."

He grinned and purposely kicked the horse's side as they headed up a hill. Chester lurched forward, throwing Clella back, and she had no choice but to grab onto Kenneth with both arms. He laughed softly.

"That's much better," he said.

"So I noticed you sat next to Eva. Where did she go in such a hurry after church?"

"Huh? Oh, Eva. I don't know. Home, I guess." He started whistling.

"She seems to like your company."

"What does that mean? I thought everybody liked my company. Don't you?" He joked, but she didn't laugh.

"I haven't had the good fortune of having it since that night of the dance," she replied.

"Are you saying you missed me?" he turned with a smirk on his face, which was way too close. Her breath caught in her throat. The gold flecks in his brown eyes sparkled in the sun. "I had a good time that night. Didn't you?" he whispered.

She looked at his lips. They drew her in like a magnet. Their faces drifted closer. Just then, Essie laughed from some distance in front of them, and the moment was lost. Clella wondered if Essie was laughing at her. *No, it's just Essie being her jovial self.* Thank heavens because Clella had almost forgotten all about Eva Hicks and Kenneth's indifference toward her since the dance. She couldn't let her defenses down that easily.

"I had a great time, Mr. Lathrom, considering it was my first dance. I'm sure there will be plenty more."

Kenneth didn't say anything. He didn't turn around or offer any explanations as to why he had been so aloof.

John Garner waited on the porch for his daughters. "We're waiting Sunday dinner for you," he called out as they approached the house. "The four of you get on in here."

As they entered the house, Hettie called from the kitchen, "Everyone, have a seat. Delphie isn't feeling well, so she went upstairs to lie down." Soon, the Garner family and their guests sat down to eat Hettie's famous fried chicken, and Clella managed to make it through the meal without speaking another word to Kenneth.

Chapter Seven

*Listen, my sons, to a father's instruction; pay
attention and gain understanding.
...Proverbs 4:1*

Kenneth, Initia, and Eric arrived at their grandpa's in record time Monday evening. Grandpa Frank hadn't been feeling well, and Initia told Kenneth she wanted to take over some soup, bread, and a freshly baked cherry pie. Grandpa Frank, like Uncle Se, possessed great wisdom, so Kenneth agreed to drive her. Right now, he could use some good advice. Eric just wanted to tag along.

When they arrived, Kenneth saw Grandpa sitting on the front porch, whittling wood and smoking his pipe. Oak and elm trees surrounded Grandpa's Ozark cabin, which he built from logs he felled near his grist mill. The water in the creek behind the cabin could be heard flowing over the rocks.

Initia kissed her grandfather on the cheek. "I brought you some stew, Grandpa."

"That's great, Honey."

Initia went on in the front door and Kenneth joined his grandfather in the other rocker on the wooden-planked porch.

"Eric, why don't you get on out there and milk those two cows," Kenneth ordered his younger brother. "I want to talk to Grandpa a minute."

"That's not fair. Why me?" Eric protested.

"It is too fair. Get on out there."

"Grandpa, now don't you tell any stories until I get back," Eric pleaded. Grandpa Frank told great stories and often sang songs of Civil War days. He was also the first man in Wright County to own a radio, though he was dead set against using fancy automobiles!

Grandpa Frank puffed on his pipe while Kenneth pulled his pipe out of his pocket. He hit it a couple of times on the porch rail before packing it with more tobacco.

"What's on your mind, Son?" Grandpa Frank asked.

Kenneth thought about Clella all the time. She even filled his dreams at night. In one dream, her dress swayed to and fro as the music played and they danced. In another, she came to him, reached out, and caressed his cheek. In perhaps the most memorable one, she came up out of the water just as she had the day of her baptism, her dress clinging to her body. She walked right into his arms and held him tight, her breasts against his chest.

"Oh, not much," Kenneth lied, and lighting his pipe, he started puffing.

Grandpa Frank set his wood down, took his pipe out of his mouth and leaned forward in his chair. "I guess I know that's not true."

Kenneth laughed. "It's a girl," he admitted. "She frustrates me so. Sometimes, I just want to wring her neck and other times, I want to plant a kiss on her so badly I can't stand it." He stood up and leaned on the porch railing.

"Well, in that case, maybe you should tell me more about her. Who is she?"

"It doesn't really matter who she is. The big question is what is she? One minute, she acts all sweet, and the next, it's like I have leprosy or something. I never know what to say."

"Well, you've never really been one at a loss for words around the ladies."

"You see, that's just it, Grandpa." Kenneth sat on the edge of the rocker and leaned closer to this man he admired. "When I'm around her, it's like I can't talk."

"I guess I know what you mean there. I felt the same way around your grandmother."

Kenneth sat back, knowing he was about to learn something very important. "What did you do?" he asked. "How did you finally talk to her enough to get married?"

Grandpa Frank started laughing and looked away as if he could see into the past. "Awe," he said, "I knew I loved your Grandma Susan very much, but I hadn't been able to tell her. I had just learned that this feller named Garner proposed to her."

"Did you say Garner?" Kenneth asked. "That's right— a guy who didn't have any problems talking to her. I didn't know what to do, but I knew I had to do something and fast. I went right over to her house. She was there and alone. I found her in one of the bedrooms, making the beds. There she stood between two of the beds with her back to me. I'll never forget how pretty she looked, her long black hair flowing in wavy curls below her waist. I pounced on her— practically tackled her right there." He chuckled.

"You didn't?"

"Yep. I took her in my arms, and I remember I said, 'Susan, don't you want to marry me instead of that other fella?' She said, 'Frank, you know I do.' I kissed her on the lips and not long after that, we were married." Grandpa Frank chuckled and looked into the distance.

"I didn't know that, Grandpa. Ever have any regrets?" Kenneth asked, even though he knew the answer. Grandma Susan died in childbirth long before Kenneth was born. Grandpa Frank never remarried. She was the love of his life. His place on Whetstone Creek became known as the "Stoney Lonesome."

"Not a one. Marriage is not a happy-ever-after, Kenny, but if you love your wife, you've done what the good book says to do."

Kenneth thought for a minute before saying, "Thanks, Grandpa. I knew talking with you would help."

"Don't know what I did. It was nothing your pa couldn't 'a done, I'm sure. Have you talked with him?"

"That's just not always easy. You know that."

"You should try harder, Kenny."

Initia came back outside. "The soup's on the stove, Grandpa," she said. "And the pie's on the table. I hope you enjoy."

Frank kissed his granddaughter on the cheek. "Thanks, Honey. That sounds mighty good." Eric brought the milk buckets in. "What did I miss? Grandpa, did you tell any stories?"

"Nothing you'd be interested in," Kenneth said and pushed his younger brother off the porch.

***

Clella gathered with the rest of the Garner girls in the parlor late Tuesday afternoon. Delphie crocheted doilies while Hettie and her other daughters stitched quilt blocks, all for their older sister, Ola, who was getting married in December.

"Now, how old is Ola?" Mag asked.

"She's twenty-six, isn't she?" Clella asked her mother.

"No, she's twenty-seven," Essie corrected. Hettie agreed with Essie.

"Well, I, for one, am glad she's getting married. I like Clarence." Mag said out of the blue. "They're a good match."

"You think so? I think they're an odd match," Clella said. "I mean I would never have put them together."

"They seem to really love each other," Essie added.

"But marriage, you know, is really a lot more than love," Hettie told her daughters. "It's a commitment and a lot of hard work." Clella pondered her mother's words.

"What do you all think of Jim?" Essie asked. "I'm very fond of him. He's so nice and a real gentleman."

"It's what *you* think that matters, Dear," Hettie answered before laying her quilting hoop down and going out to the kitchen. Mag followed her, asking if she could have an oatmeal cookie.

"I think he's a very good guy," Clella said. "Although, I can't say much for the company he keeps."

"You mean Kenny? Clella, why don't you just ask him if he's seeing Eva Hicks? If he says no, then ask him why he didn't come see you after the dance." Essie's eyes sparkled and she laughed gently. "After all, the most he can say is yes and then you'll know."

"I don't have to ask him, because I don't care. I've thought about it and the best thing for me to do is forget about him. I couldn't care less."

They all heard a vehicle pull in the drive, but it didn't sound like the Garners' car. Then the horn sounded— AH-OOO-GA. Essie stood up first and went to the window.

"It's him. It's Kenny."

Clella's pulse instantly raced and butterflies danced in her stomach. Her hands trembled with excitement, but her face reddened in anger *What's he doing here?* Kenneth knocked on the door.

"Get the door," Essie told Clella.

"I'm not getting the door. You get the door."

Essie laughed. "I'm not getting the door. You answer it." Essie pushed Clella toward the door, but Clella dug in her heels. Kenneth knocked again. The two sisters each tried to force the other one, turning circles and getting nowhere.

"Oh, for heaven's sake," Delphie said, putting her crocheting down. "I'll get the door."

Just then, Hettie appeared from the kitchen and gave her girls a questioning look. "What is going on in here?" she asked as she opened it herself.

"Kenneth. What a pleasant surprise! Come on in."

"May I talk with Clella, Mrs. Garner?"

"She's in the parlor." She motioned with her arm and his eyes followed. All three girls froze in place and stared at him. He took off his hat.

"Clella, Kenneth would like to talk with you," Hettie announced before returning to the kitchen. Clella released her grip, giving Essie an unexpected foothold; as Essie pushed, Clella suddenly lunged forward toward her guest.

"What do you want?" Clella asked.

"I," he fumbled with his hat and cleared his throat. "I had some time today and thought you might like to go for a driving lesson."

"I don't think so. It's getting late and I should really help Momma with dinner."

"I can help her," Essie quickly said. "You go ahead."

Oh, great! Clella was beginning to think that somehow Essie and Kenneth planned this. It didn't help matters that he stood there with his hat in hand and the top button of his shirt unbuttoned. She couldn't stop staring at his dark features, and as much as she liked to pretend she didn't want to see him, deep down, her heart betrayed her.

"Well, we won't be long, will we?" she asked.

"It all depends on how fast you learn," he replied. "If grade school is any indication, it shouldn't take long at all." He smiled and she did, too, realizing he'd paid her a compliment. With Clella in the driver's seat, Kenneth began to explain which pedals were the clutch, the brake, and the gas. He put his arm around on the back of her seat.

"Now, you push in on the gas and let out on the clutch." As Clella attempted to do as he instructed, the truck lurched and sputtered.

"Easy," Kenneth said. After a moment, he softened his raised voice. "Slowly."

"I'm trying." She let out on the clutch, but the truck died. "I can't do this." Clella threw her hands in the air and sighed.

"Yes you can. Try it again." The truck lurched and sputtered, but this time, Clella managed to let the clutch out and move it forward as she gave it gas. She looked at Kenneth and they both laughed. She was driving! The truck gained speed as it went along.

"Shift gears," Kenneth ordered. "How?" she gasped.

"Push in on the clutch." She hesitated, trying to remember the clutch. When she pushed down, the engine roared.

"Let up on the gas," Kenneth yelled at her. There was an awful metal grinding sound as she tried to find second gear. "Stop!" he hollered.

"Quit yelling at me!" she cried. The engine died again.

"I'm not..." he shouted, but then lowered his voice. "I'm not yelling at you."

"This was a bad idea." She opened the door. "I'll walk home." She threw open the door and jumped out of the truck.

"Clella, wait a minute." Kenneth slammed the door and left the vehicle in the middle of the dirt road. She briskly walked away. He ran after her. Grabbing her elbow, he swung her around to face him, but before he could say anything, she jerked her arm free.

"I should never have listened to Essie." Clella spit the words out rapid fire. "I should never have gone to that dance with you. You and your acting all nice, when all the time you were just wanting to be with Eva Hicks. What are you even doing here?"

Kenneth frowned. "What are you talking about?"

"I didn't even see you the whole month of September until my birthday, but I overheard Eva at church talking about you and Friday nights." She rolled her eyes and raised her hands. "I must be crazy." She whirled around and started walking off again.

Kenneth stood there contemplating everything she just said. His eyes widened as realization sank in. *It was jealousy. She...was jealous.* Finally, he called after her. "Do you *like* me?"

She didn't turn or miss a step, but kept right on walking. "No!" she yelled emphatically.

But he didn't need any more encouragement. He ran after her and practically tackled her. Grasping her shoulders, he spun her around.

She tried to wriggle free, but his gaze caught hers. It spoke volumes and held her spellbound. There was no teasing in his eyes—just truth. He gently reached out and traced the outline of her face. Then, he brushed strands of wayward hair from the middle of her forehead, following them down to hold the tip of her brown locks in the palm of his hand, staring at them as if they were a priceless treasure. Her breath caught in her throat and her heart raced wildly.

He spoke, slowly letting his eyes drift to meet hers. "There's...only ever been one girl for me, and...I'm looking at her." He lifted her chin and kissed her, lingering sweetly on her lips. He pulled her close, clutching her in his embrace. Without realizing it, she clung to him. Time stopped. Nothing else existed except the two of them and a mutual heavenly intimacy. She could deny it no more. She loved him.

Clella broke the kiss to look into his eyes. She needed reassurance that he also felt this overwhelming sensation that everything was finally right—that the two of them were meant for each other. She found all the truth in the windows to his soul.

He hugged her tightly and whispered in her ear, "I love you, Clella."

Happiness like she had never known swept over her. "I love you, too," she softly replied.

He suddenly picked her up and swung her around and around. When he put her down, his eyes danced teasingly. "You want to get married?"

"To whom, you?" she playfully answered.

"Well, you could marry the King of Spain, but I'm a little more available. Better looking, too!"

"But why should I marry you?"

"Because you love me!"

She wrapped her arms around his neck and smiled. "I do, don't I?"

AH-OOO-GA. The horn of a car unable to pass on the road sounded, and they both ran back to the truck laughing and holding hands.

Clella slid across the seat first and let Kenneth get behind the wheel. She could learn to drive some other time. For now, she just wanted to be next to him. Between shifting gears, he wrapped his arm around her protectively. They stole glances at each other as he drove. She couldn't quit smiling. Twice he even bent his head and kissed her lightly. Once, he threw his head back and laughed.

"What?" Clella asked, laughing, too.

"I can't believe you love me! I thought you hated me."

"Well, you have to admit you've been pretty incorrigible! You used to tease me something awful in grade school."

He squeezed her hand. "The prettiest girl in all of Wright County and she loves me."

"Yea, well, what about you? You're quite the ladies' man around Hartville. Am I going to have to beat them off with a stick?"

"You'd do that for me?" he teased her. He parked the truck in her front yard and turned to face her.

"You bet," she said. "Someone's going to have to tell Eva Hicks to find herself another beau."

He kissed her again. His eyes twinkled as he said, "You haven't answered my question."

Smiling slyly, she looked at him and asked, "Why, what question was that, Mr. Lathrom?"

He sighed, but went ahead and took the bait. He cleared his throat and sat up straight in the seat. Lifting her hand, he looked her in the eyes and said, "Clella Garner, will you marry me?" His hand shook slightly, but his voice resonated strongly with love.

"You know I will," she answered and this time she kissed him.

That night, before her head rested on her pillow, Clella knelt beside her bed and thanked God for this sweet love He had given her. Then she blew out the lamp and crawled into bed beside Essie.

"I can't believe it," Essie whispered. "You're going to be Mrs. Kenneth Lathrom."

Clella smiled.

Chapter Eight

*Therefore shall a man leave his father and his
mother, and shall cleave unto his wife and
they shall be one flesh.
......Genesis 2:24 KJV*

The winter of 1929 dumped an abundance of snow on Wright County, making it necessary on many occasions for Jim and Kenneth to hitch up the sleigh in order to take the girls for rides through the glistening frozen countryside. The sleigh bells jingled as each couple held hands and cuddled close.

Despite the bitter cold, Clella glowed with the warmth of happiness, and she wasn't the only one: Essie and Jim also decided to tie the knot. Jim surprised Essie, as well as Kenneth and Clella, on one of their outings when he pulled from his pocket an important document concerning a parcel of land off Highway 38 not too far from Hartville.

"What's this?" Essie asked.

"It's our loan!" he answered with pride. "I'm buying our land." They all stared at the signatures. Sure enough, it was official and signed by Laura Ingalls Wilder, the treasurer of the Federal Reserve Bank in Mansfield.

February, however, was one of mixed blessings for the whole Garner household. First, the news came that their beloved Artie went home to be with the Lord. She no longer suffered and they could rejoice in that. Clella remembered her mother's words, "the Lord giveth and the Lord taketh away." And then the Lord blesses new beginnings as Jim and Essie married toward the end of the month.

Delphie, Clella, and Mag were the only Garner children remaining at home now. March and April seemed to pass quickly. Clella and Kenneth spent more and more time at the Lathroms'.

News of Kenneth's engagement to Clella pleased De.

"He finally approves of something I've done," Kenneth told his sister one evening while he, Clella, and Initia sat on the front porch. He smiled at Clella.

"Honestly, Kenneth," Initia said, "I think you have this tremendous chip on your shoulder."

Kenneth started to say something, but just then, De and Grandpa Frank walked out the front door. Grandpa coughed and hacked. He looked even frailer than before.

"Kenneth," he said, and then coughed again. "You know I own that little parcel of land just north of town?"

"Yeah, Grandpa?"

"Well, your father and I have been talking. You and your lovely bride-to-be here are welcome to make your start there," he offered.

"Grandpa, are you sure?" Kenneth asked excitedly. He hadn't been as fortunate as Jim in securing a home site. He and Eric were so busy plowing, planting, and splitting rails that there hadn't been any time for planning his future.

Clella stood up next to Kenneth, slipping her hand through his arm. "That's so wonderful of you, Mr. Lathrom," and she kissed the older gentlemen on the cheek.

"I like her, Son," he said to Kenneth. "You'd better marry her quick before she changes her mind!"

Kenneth put his arm around Clella, "I'm inclined to agree with you, Grandpa." They all laughed.

"That's what I told him," De added. "We've got to help them get started."

Kenneth and Clella worked hastily to get a crop in before the end of planting season. He plowed and she planted. Working together even before marriage, they were both so full of hope and love.

***

The 4th of July festivities were scheduled all day on the courthouse lawn in the middle of town. Clella had a great time. She and Kenneth danced, lost the three-legged race, and ate ice cream cones at the ice cream parlor on the north side of the square. Later, they watched fireworks along with Jim and Essie.

It was late before she got home, but her mother waited up for her in the parlor. "Oh, Mama, we had such a good time. You should have come, too." She walked closer to her mother.

"Why are you crying, Mama?"

Hettie began crying even more. "It's Delphie," she managed, but then stopped. Delphie suffered epileptic seizures and Clella knew anything could've happened. She knelt before her mother.

"What, Mama? What happened?"

Hettie shook her head. "Oh, Clella, Delphie's pregnant!"

"What?" At first, Clella thought maybe she didn't hear correctly. Delphie wasn't seeing anyone. "Mama, I don't understand. Who?"

"Do you remember that young traveling salesman passing through a few weeks back?"

Clella vaguely remembered him. "Maybe. He was in town for a few days, wasn't he?"

"Yes, and Delphie was quite taken with him."

"Oh, Mama, don't say that."

Hettie nodded again and couldn't stop crying.

Clella sat down and asked, "Does Papa know?"

"Yes. He's so angry with her. I think he blames me."

Her mother looked so burdened. Clella reached out and hugged her.

Clella couldn't sleep that night. She tossed and turned, worrying about Delphie. Already, their neighbors considered Delphie strange because of her seizures, which would occur without notice. Her body would stiffen and shake and she would fall to the floor, but now with the pregnancy, Delphie would be ridiculed, and her family would be the gossip of the town.

Beyond that, Clella wondered what complication epilepsy might cause during pregnancy. She thought about the handful of women she knew who had died during childbirth. Even Kenneth's mother died shortly after giving birth to Initia.

As time passed, though, the Garner family, John, Hettie, and all their children, began to embrace the idea of this new little life growing inside Delphie. They were strong and would stand by her and each other through whatever may come.

***

Kenneth and Clella married on August 13th. She wore a simple dress of white linen and lace. Kenny thought she looked like a vision from a dream as her dad walked her down the aisle. While Essie held her bouquet, Clella turned to take Kenneth's hand, and together, they said their vows. Later, when he picked her up and carried her over the threshold of their new home, even he was a little nervous.

"Welcome home, Mrs. Lathrom," he said as he put her back on her feet.

"Why thank you, Mr. Lathrom." He watched her take a quick glance around. Red chintz curtains hung on the only window in the kitchen. Two fine wooden rockers sat on each side of the woven rug in front of the fireplace.

She smiled at him and wrapped her arms around his neck. "So, this is what married life is like!"

His eyes twinkled. "No...not yet."

She let out a squeal as he whisked her back off her feet, entered the bedroom and tossed her onto the bed. She giggled as he closed the door.

He lay beside her and tenderly brushed her hair away from her face. "I've dreamed of this night. I want to fall asleep every night holding you in my arms."

"Oh, Kenneth, is this real?" Her fingers traced the outline of his lips. "I love you so much." He kissed her and they floated into a dimension beyond the room, beyond now, and into a place where there were only the two of them, and they were one.

Their beginning was humble. The "old Grandpa place," as their home fondly became known, had three small rooms. Uncle Se gave them a milk cow, and John and Hettie Garner gave them two calves. Their families and friends gave from what they had to help out the newlyweds.

They had no well, so Clella walked down the hill to the spring and drew water in buckets. Of course, when she walked downhill, the buckets were empty, but when she went uphill, they were heavy and full!

In the middle of the day, as Kenneth worked in the fields, he would remove his hat and blot the sweat away with his handkerchief. That's when she would cross the field with a bucket in hand. He always kissed her first and then drank from the ladle she gave him. Then, he would lovingly caress her chin or the outline of her face.

The thrill of each sunset was when he entered their home and smelled Clella's cooking. He would sneak up behind her and kiss her neck, and she would turn to face him and giggle. He would laugh, and even though their backs hurt and their muscles ached, it didn't matter, because they were alone sharing the privacy of their home.

In the mornings, while it was still dark, they would wake in each other's arms, neither wishing to relinquish ecstasy. But, Daisy would moo and the rooster would crow, and they could no longer delay the inevitable.

Clella would put the coffee on while Kenneth poured water from the pitcher into the washbasin, and another day would begin.

The garden yielded a fine crop, the peach trees bore fruit, the apple trees bloomed, and their love flourished like a well-tended vine. And that wasn't all.

***

And God blessed them, saying, be fruitful and multiply.
......Genesis 1:22 KJV

October 28, 1929

"Mama, how have you done it all these years?" Clella asked Hettie as the two of them prepared her father's birthday dinner. "I work from sunup till sundown and more. I know you did, but you also had all of us children to take care of. I don't even have children."

Hettie continued rolling dough to make crusts for the pies she intended to bake. "Honey, you just do what you have to do. God never gives you more than you can handle."

"It's just that sometimes I get so weak, and lately, I've been a little dizzy."

Her mother stopped and glanced up at her with scrutiny. "Hand me the flour," Hettie ordered and then added, "hmm."

Clella turned around and reached for the sack of flour on the Hoosier cabinet, "You know, Mother, I don't have a rolling pin. I have all this fruit and I try to make pies, but it's really hard to make good crust without a rolling pin." She handed Hettie the flour, but her mother didn't appear to be listening to her. "What?" Clella asked. "What is it?"

"Oh, nothing, Dear." Hettie turned her attention back to the crusts, but asked, "Have you been sick to your stomach lately?"

"No, not really. But I could eat a horse!"

"Hmm!" Hettie picked up a stack of plates.

"Here, set the table. I'm sure the others will start arriving at any minute."

More voices could be heard from the parlor as Hettie and Clella started carrying dishes of food from the kitchen to the table. Essie and Jim arrived.

"Happy Birthday, Dad." Essie told her father as she gave him a big hug.

How nice to have so many of her family together, Clella thought as they all sat down and gave thanks. Everyone visited and enjoyed dinner. Delphie suddenly shocked everyone as she kicked back her chair and dashed out the back door. All could hear the unmistakable sounds of a dinner refusing to stay down– one of the joys of pregnancy.

At that time, Clella finally understood her mother's earlier questions. She glanced at her mother who laughed and said something to Essie.

She then looked at Kenneth. He was so handsome. She didn't hear any of the conversation. Instead, she contemplated the possibility of her own motherhood. Yes, that must be it. She was pregnant. Excitement washed over her.

After dinner, Clella helped clean up. She worked the handle of the pump up and down, squirting water in the sink and over the dishes.

"I sure wish we had a well and water pumped in the house," she said, without realizing she had interrupted a conversation between Hettie, Essie, and Delphie. Everyone froze and stared at her in disbelief. "What?" she asked, shrugging her shoulders.

"Clella, have you heard anything I just said?" Essie asked.

"Don't mind her, Dear. Clella is just figuring out she's pregnant."

"What? Do you mean?" With a swift motion, Clella shushed her and Essie stopped.

"Kenneth doesn't know. As a matter of fact, I can't wait to go home and tell him." She couldn't stop smiling.

"The two of you don't have any money in Hartville Bank, do you?" Essie asked.

"Well, it's not much, but we're doing okay."

"You *weren't* listening to me!" Essie exclaimed. "You'd better get over there first thing in the morning and make a withdrawal."

Hettie spoke next, "Now, Essie, you're really overreacting."

"No, I'm not. Have you been listening to the radio?"

"What are you talking about?" Clella asked.

"The stock market has been all over the news."

Clella didn't understand much about the stock market. "What does that have to do with our money in Hartville Bank?"

"Jim's been reading about it. It seems that the banks may have invested people's money in the market, which is dropping rapidly. We're going to withdraw our account tomorrow."

Just then, the women heard the radio as the men increased the volume. They all laid their towels down and joined the men in the parlor.

The newscaster spoke clearly. "After last Thursday's bleak day at the New York Stock Exchange, investors were still optimistic as a result of the involvement of the bankers, but today's exchange is bleaker still. Richard Whitney, the acting president of the New York Stock Exchange, didn't even make an appearance on Wall Street today, and the Exchange closed, leaving no hope for a rebound. Many believe we could be at the beginning of a national disaster of great proportions."

Jim and John were probably the only ones in the room who understood, at least in part, the current happenings of the stock market. At the time, though, none of them could imagine the far reaching repercussions of that day.

Later that night, Kenneth walked into their dimly lit bedroom. Clella, already dressed in a sheer linen nightgown with tiny pink roses, turned from the bureau and looked at him teasingly. She couldn't keep her mouth straight, though she tried.

"What are you smiling about?" he asked. "You look like you're hiding a secret or something."

"Maybe I am."

He laughed. "You'd better tell me or I'll tickle you 'til you do." She screamed and giggled as he wrapped his arms around her and the tips of his fingers found her sensitive areas. They fell on the bed together, laughing and wriggling.

"Okay. Okay. I'll tell you," she surrendered. When he released her, he traced her cheek with his hand and he softly kissed her lips. Then he looked into her eyes, waiting.

Clella beamed as she told him, "We're going to have a baby!"

Chapter Nine

*Rejoice in the Lord always, and again I say
rejoice.
......Philippians 4:4 KJV*

Kenneth dusted his hat before placing it on his head and walking out the front door into the morning. He stood on the porch in the brisk autumn air and looked out over the hills. The trees, still painted with color, outlined the recently harvested and barren field. He looked toward the barn where just yesterday he put in the last of the hay and he noticed the roof needed repair before winter set in. A group of cackling geese flew in a "V" formation overhead.

The door opened behind him. Clella held his jacket in her hand. "I thought you might need this." She smiled and kissed him.

"You sure you don't want to go with me?" he asked.

"No, I've got too much to do today. Don't forget to pick up some sugar, though."

As she turned, he caught her hand. "You take it easy. Remember, you're going to have our son."

She hugged him. "I'll be fine...and you mean daughter, don't you?"

"Don't you be havin' no girl."

She laughed and closed the door on her way back inside.

Kenneth climbed in the truck and started toward town. On his way, he thought about Clella and the baby. He felt excited, proud, and worried all at the same time. He grinned. *I'm going to be a Dad!* Then, he frowned. *Will everything be okay?*

Diane Yates

His mother died after giving birth to Initia when he was very young, but he could still remember how much it hurt. What if Clella died?

As he rounded the curve by Miller's pond, he saw people lined up all around Hartville Square. Never had he seen such a crowd for no apparent reason. He parked and went inside Hattie's General Store. He tipped his hat to the girl behind the counter, "How do, Ora? What's all the fuss about outside?"

"Everybody's trying to get their money out of the bank. I got mine out this morning."

"Why would everybody want to do that?" he asked, but thought about the conversation he, Jim, and John had last night after hearing the news. He continued perusing the shelves for the items he needed, though, and told Ora, "I need some sugar."

She turned to get the sugar. "There's a rumor that the bank doesn't have enough money. You want ten or twenty pounds?"

"Better give me twenty." With renewed interest, he glanced outside the window at the crowd.

He left the store and started toward the bank with concern etched on his face, but as he drew closer, he noticed people starting to leave. Some seemed mad, others stunned. He noticed the window shade at the bank being pulled down behind the sign that read "Closed". Worried, he grabbed Artis Groves's arm. "What's going on, Artis?"

"The bank's out of money. They just closed their doors." Artis stared into the distance. "Every penny I had was in there."

"Yeah, but they're going to open back up tomorrow, right?"

"I don't think so, Kenneth. What am I going to tell Goldie?" Artis walked away despondently.

Kenneth swallowed hard. He intended to make a withdrawal today. They needed that money to put in supplies for winter. What was going on? He decided to return home and planned to turn on that new radio he and Clella bought just last week. In fact, if they hadn't, he would've had enough money to get what they needed.

Later, he and Clella listened to the radio and heard about the masses of people who lost large sums of money because of the stock market. From New York to San Francisco and all parts in between, the crash of a once booming market devastated the country. By the end of October, the news reported the month's losses for the market were sixteen billion dollars. Neither Kenneth nor Clella realized how this would directly affect their area.

In the days and weeks to come, there were countless stories all across the United States of people committing suicide because of their distress. In Hartville and the surrounding towns, commodities were soon depleted, as replenishments simply didn't come. What few companies existed in the area soon closed, and many people found themselves unemployed. Kenneth was glad he had bought twenty pounds of sugar that day instead of ten, because Hattie's shelves were now mostly bare, and she had been completely out of sugar for some time. The radio he and Clella bought proved to be the last major purchase they would make for a very long time. The bank remained closed, and it turned out they did lose their money.

At the end of each day, though, Clella amazed him. No matter how bare their cupboard, she managed to cook a meal fit for a king– or at the very least, the two of them. It was truly her gift, like magic or something.

He would sit down and she would wrap her arms around him from behind and whisper in his ear, "Everything's going to be all right, Dear." In that moment, he found the courage to keep going.

One November day, Kenneth was splitting rails to put away firewood before the first real cold spell. He began to wonder about matters how they were going to make it.

Clella had canned fruits and vegetables, the chickens laid eggs, and Daisy provided milk. Being pregnant, Clella needed to take care of herself. He knew that.

One right after another, he placed a log on its end, then swung the ax up and back down, splitting the log in half. He had to store enough firewood for the cook stove and to keep them warm.

Their few head of cattle would have to make it with a little bit of hay and corn. If need be, they could butcher a calf and a chicken or two, but no one knew what would happen next spring. He placed another log on end, up with the ax and back down, splitting it in half. When they needed seed, would it be available? If so, would it be too expensive? Where were they going to get the money?

Again his arm went up with the ax, but his mind drifted and the ax drifted too. As he threw his weight behind the crushing blow, the ax struck the wood off center before landing across the top of his left foot.

Kenneth yelled out in pain and disbelief. Blood splattered, and he dropped the ax, before falling down.

Clella must have seen the whole thing from the kitchen window. Almost instantly, she dashed out the front door.

"Oh, my God. Kenneth? Kenneth?"

"I'm okay," he managed, wincing with each word. Clella wasted no time. She said nothing, but took her apron off and started tearing it into strips. She knelt down and tied them tight around his foot.

She was so calm, but biting her lower lip. Her brown hair fell in soft locks around her shoulders. She helped him up and got him to the truck. She then climbed in and drove him straight to Doc Latimer's in town. He didn't need to remind her to shift or turn. In fact, she drove perfectly.

Luckily, Doc was in his office, located in the downstairs of his house. He stitched Kenneth up before telling him, "I don't think you'll be chopping anymore wood this year."

Great! Kenneth took a deep breath and blew it out. This wasn't what he wanted to hear. Now what would he do?

Two days later, as he hobbled around the house on crutches, he took a cylindrical piece of wood that was just perfect for what he had in mind. He leaned his crutches in the corner, sat down in front of the fireplace, and started whittling and sanding.

At first, Clella didn't realize what he was making, but after a while, she sat down across from him and grinned. "You're making me a rolling pin!" He didn't look at her, but kept his concentration on the wood. "Yep, how else am I going to get you to bake me a pie?"

"Don't be ridiculous," she scolded him. "We're almost out of flour." He glanced at her and the two of them laughed. They had no money, almost no staples, and Kenneth was nursing a foot he almost cut in half, but somehow, they kept a sense of humor. She kissed his cheek.

The next couple of months, Clella carried water up the hill from the spring, milked the cow in the morning and evening, carried in firewood, fed the livestock, and did all of Kenneth's other chores as well as her own.

One evening, after Clella returned from the spring, she entered the house, huffing and puffing, like always. "Can't we dig a well? The Jones have one, and Essie and Jim too."

Kenneth stopped whittling and pointed to his foot. "I can't exactly dig one right now, Clella." He knew she wanted a well. How could he not? She mentioned it every day!

"I know, but promise me as soon as we can, we'll have one dug."

He decided not to say more. Instead, he cocked his head to one side, tossed his piece of wood back on the pile, and put away his knife.

As Clella grew bigger, more and more the words she spoke seemed like nagging. Thank God his foot was almost healed. At least he could pace a bit while she complained. The winter had been bitterly cold, but spring would be here soon. He looked forward to getting out of the house just as soon as he could!

Chapter Ten

*Lo children are an heritage of the Lord: and
the fruit of the womb is His reward.
.....Psalms 127:3 KJV*

The wood burning in the fireplace warmed the Garners' parlor. It was just like old times: the Garner sisters sat together with their mother, working on quilt blocks and knitting for Delphie's baby, who was due next month. Commodities were scarce, so when they ran out of material and yarn, they resorted to making quilt blocks out of old clothes and reused wool from tattered sweaters and shawls.

"I'm feeling pretty good," Delphie said. "I'm huge, but thankful I'm having a good day."

"It shouldn't be much longer, now," Clella told Delphie.

"What do you think, Mom?" Essie asked, "Three or four weeks?"

Hettie looked above her spectacles at Delphie. "Well, I certainly don't think it'll be any longer than that, but you can't always tell."

"Oh, I can't wait to have a baby here." Mag jumped out of her chair with such excitement she practically dropped the quilt blocks she cut. "Can you teach me how to knit, Delphie? I want to knit the baby something."

"Yes," Delphie answered. "But what are you going to make? I think it's going to be a girl."

"Oh, no, I think it's going to be a boy," put in Clella.

"Have you had a dream about the baby?" Hettie asked. "Because you know what they say: if you dream about your baby, whatever it is in your dream, whether a boy or a girl, that's what it'll be."

"Was it like that for you, Mama, with us?" Clella asked. "Did you dream of all of us girls?"

"I'm not sure about that," Hettie used her teeth to cut her sewing thread in two, "but I do know I had dreams about the boys–all two of them!" The girls laughed.

All through March, the wind blew strong, cardinals and red-breasted robins reclaimed their territory, and the tulips bloomed. April finally arrived along with the day for little Hobart Lee Garner to enter the world. After Delphie's difficult delivery, and everyone heard his tiny cry, they all oohed and aahed, anxious to hold the newborn. He was a precious bundle, despite the large strawberry birthmark covering almost half of his face. Grandpa Garner, who was quite taken with him, soon gave him a nickname that stuck. Everyone called him "Dude".

***

May 17, 1930

Kenneth sat on the edge of his chair, then got up and paced back and forth before sitting back down again. He stood when Hettie came out of the bedroom.

"Everything's going to be all right," she assured him, but just then Clella cried out and Hettie rushed back into the room.

Kenneth paced up and down, back and forth. He looked at the clock. It had been thirteen hours and fifty minutes since Clella's labor began. Would she really be all right? What if something happened? He felt so helpless. He kept thinking about his own mother. One day she was there and expecting a baby. The next day she was gone, leaving baby Initia to keep them awake at night with her crying.

Kenneth stopped pacing, sat down, and put his face in his hands. Five minutes passed. Then, he heard the faintest little cry, coming from the bedroom. He couldn't stand it anymore. He threw open the door.

"It's a boy!" Hettie said as she handed him a bundle in a blanket with its tiny face exposed and wrinkled in a shrill cry of protest. Inside the blanket, he kicked his legs vigorously, just like he had for the last few months. He had a full head of dark hair and was the sweetest thing Kenneth had ever seen. With utter wonder, Kenneth turned to Clella. Her hair was matted, and sweat moistened her face. She looked tired, but never had she looked more beautiful to him.

"Are you all right?" he asked her.

"I'm fine," she answered. And she was fine. She was amazing. She didn't die. He knew now he didn't have to worry about her. She could do anything!

***

Propped up in bed, Clella smiled as she watched her husband with their firstborn son. It had been a long road–a tough road. It didn't help that money, food, and even the most necessary staples were hard to come by.

When Kenneth hurt his foot, she assumed so many of the daily chores. Her back ached fiercely at times and she would lie on the floor just to relieve the pressure, but looking at her boys now made it all worthwhile. Kenneth handed her son to her and kissed her on the forehead.

"So I guess next time you can have a girl if you want," he told her. His eyes beamed and she could read the depth of his love there.

"That's awfully big of you to give me your permission!" She chided him, smiling because her heart was full of love.

***

In the heat of the sun, Kenneth took his handkerchief and wiped the sweat from his brow. Then he swung the reigns over his shoulder and took up the plow again. He didn't even notice his row becoming a little uneven.

Wow, a son, he thought. He was a father. He could hardly believe it. Little Wallace, now three days old, woke up at various times during the night, crying for sustenance. Even though only Clella could meet his need, Kenneth couldn't help but wake up also. He wanted to see him, hold him, and watch his little, heaven-sent miracle. This tiny baby transformed him and Clella from husband and wife into a family.

Most of their relatives had already been by to see the baby– Grandpa Frank, Mom and Dad Garner, Uncle Se, and Clella's sisters. Even Kenneth's Dad, De, wasted no time in coming to visit his new grandson. As Kenneth watched the tenderness with which his father held Wallace, he couldn't help but see his father differently. Gone were the stern lines in his father's face, now replaced by smiles, laughter, and pride. It made Kenneth feel good. It was strange how it took the birth of his son to somehow establish the bond between his dad and him, a bond he craved as a child. De always had been closer to either Aubrey, the oldest, or Eric, the youngest, or Initia, the only girl. Kenneth was the one who wasn't smart enough. No matter how hard he worked, his dad seemed more impressed with the others.

The horse whinnied. "Whoa." Kenneth looked back at the day's progress and shook his head in disappointment. The May sun sat a little higher in the sky, but nevertheless, it was about quitting time.

Clella managed to set the table and take the last of their warmed up supper off the wood stove before the baby started crying. When Kenneth came through the door, she was situated in the wooden rocker Grandpa Frank gave them, preparing to nurse the baby.

"Supper's ready," she called out to him. "Go ahead and wash up and start without me." Before Kenneth went to the kitchen, he came to her and kissed their son, then placed a light kiss on her forehead. He smiled and rubbed his finger along the baby's cheek, before looking at Clella.

"I love you," he said. Their eyes met. Her heart couldn't have held more love for him than she felt right at that moment. She smiled. No words could communicate better than the language in each other's eyes.

"Go on and wash up," she told him softly. "I think Jim and Essie are stopping by."

"Again? I think they've been here every day since he was born," he called out from the washstand.

"Are you complaining?" She wanted to laugh, but kept her voice even and low.

"No, it's not that."

"Besides, I thought you really liked Essie's fresh baked bread," she said quietly because Wallace had fallen asleep after eating.

"Oh, I do."

Clella placed the sleeping baby in his crib and joined her husband at the table. Kenneth spread butter on a slice of bread.

"And that's fresh churned butter Essie brought us," she gave him a pointed look.

"Forget I said anything," he smiled. "It's just surprises me, you know."

"I know."

"I mean, how can they find the time? It's planting season." He dipped out a helping of vegetable stew.

Clella placed a hand on his arm. "Essie wants to get pregnant more than anything. They really want a child of their own."

"I know Jim does."

"Have you seen how she wants to hold Wallace all the time when she's here? I feel so badly for her."

"I'm sure it's just a matter of time."

Clella removed their plates as Kenneth drained the last of his milk glass. She wanted to get the dishes done before Jim and Essie arrived.

"Any coffee?" he asked.

"Not tonight. We're running low and Hattie's has been out for some time now."

"Well then," he rose and went out on the porch. It was a beautiful evening. Clella joined Kenneth.

Soon the dust stirred and the Model A pulled in the yard. When Jim and Essie got out, Essie carried a jug in her hands.

"Here's some fresh churned buttermilk," she said.

"Wonderful!" Clella smiled as she and Kenneth exchanged glances. She took the milk from her sister. "I don't know what I would do if it weren't for you, Essie." Inside, Essie hovered over the baby.

"Don't you wake him up! He'll wake up soon enough," Clella scolded her.

Essie looked at her with a twinkle in her eye. "Now, surely it wouldn't hurt if I just picked him up and cuddled him a little, now would it?"

Clella held her hand up. "Don't you dare!"

Essie chuckled. A moment later, her face straightened and she stared into the distance. "Oh, Clella, why can't I have a baby?"

Clella hugged her sister. "You will, Essie. Just give it time."

Chapter Eleven

And my God will meet all your needs
according to his glorious riches in Christ Jesus.
.....Philippians 4:19

Clella regained her figure over the summer months. Though her son required so much of her time, the chores still needed to be done as well. It was hot and dry–too dry.

One evening, as Clella put away the supper dishes, Kenneth approached her from behind. He moved her hair back off the side of her neck and kissed her soft skin. She turned and their lips met. As he pulled her closer to him, there was a knock at the door.

Kenneth opened the door to a man with a straggly beard and strong odor. His tattered shirt hung loosely on his thin body, and his stringy blonde hair matted in clumps where it needed cleaning. "Sir, do you have any work I can do?" the man asked. "I'm really hungry."

"Sorry," Kenneth answered. "I do all the work around here myself."

"Just wait and I'll get you some ham and biscuits," Clella said.

The man's hands shook slightly, but he grinned from ear to ear. "Much obliged, Ma'am."

In a moment, Clella returned with a cloth sack containing a helping of ham and biscuits. "God bless you, Sir," she told him. She knew he was a vagabond, but wherever he laid his head tonight, she wanted his stomach to be full.

"I don't think we can feed every stranger that knocks on our door," Kenneth said after the man left.

"Maybe not, but I doubt we'll miss that little bit of food too much," she answered. In truth, neither knew what tomorrow would bring.

The next day, Kenneth took Clella and the baby to her folks in Competition. She and Essie were going to help their mother put away peaches as they did every September. Even Mag and Delphie joined in. As the five of them sat in the kitchen and peeled several bushels of peaches from the Garners' fruit trees, Clella smiled. It seemed just like old times again. The only differences were little "Dude" and Wallace waking every two to three hours for feedings.

"Can I hold the baby, Clella?" Mag asked.

"Sure you can."

"Not until we're all finished here," Hettie said. "You're not going to get out of work that easily, young lady."

Mag bit into one of the peach slices. "Yum, these are really sweet."

"Good," Clella said. "Because we don't have much sugar to put in them."

The general store in Hartville, like all over the country, rationed out sugar and other commodities in order to meet the demand with limited supplies.

Just then, Delphie's bowl fell to the floor with an awful clang, spilling sliced peaches everywhere. Her chair fell backward, hitting the floor with a thud and Delphie's body stiffened as her eyes glazed over. Before anyone could react, the knife she held grazed her forearm. Clella quickly retrieved the knife and placed a dishcloth over the wound as Hettie managed to get a spoon into her daughter's mouth to protect her tongue as Delphie started jerking.

When Dude began crying, Mag lifted him into her arms. Delphie lost control of her bladder.

Essie, who had been trying to stay out of the way, said, "I'll get a change of clothes and a towel."

After the seizure ended, they all helped Delphie get cleaned up.

While Delphie rested, they finished canning the peaches. Later, Clella and Essie walked down to the creek. The water gently trickled over the rocks and sand. The birds sang as they flew in and out of the green brush.

"Have you talked to Mother any about Delphie?" Essie asked.

"No, but did you notice her seizure seemed longer?"

"Yes. Mother is quite concerned about her. So much so, she and Dad are considering sending her to a sanitarium in Springfield."

"But...but, how?" Clella was shocked. "What about Dude?"

"Mother'll take care of him."

"I just can't believe it." They rounded the end of the fence posts and headed back toward their parents' home.

"Doc Latimer says there's a doctor in Springfield that's trying some new treatments. Maybe he can help Delphie."

"That would be good. Oh, I do hope so." Clella said.

"Besides," Essie continued, "Mom doesn't look any too well herself."

"When are they thinking about doing this?" Clella asked.

"I don't know. Mom doesn't really want to, but Dad's insisting." As they approached the house, Essie whispered, "Don't say anything. Let Mom tell you when she's ready." Clella nodded.

They entered the house just in time to hear Mag protesting. "When are things going to get better?" Mag whined. "I just want everything like it used to be before this old depression."

"You know those on the radio say it's liable to get much worse before it gets better," Essie said.

Clella raised her hands and exclaimed, "How can it get much worse?"

Essie laughed. "Well, I suppose we could have no sugar at all!"

Clella sighed, knowing her sister was right. She nodded, "I guess I should be thankful for what I do have." Wallace cried as he woke up from his nap and Kenneth pulled up outside.

***

Besides enduring hard economic times, the extremely cold temperatures of the winter of '32 seemed to last forever. The hot, dry summer before had taken its toll on crops, making food even more scarce. With spring came the return of bluebirds and the opening of the last of the peaches, apples, and cherries.

One sunny day in the last part of March, Wallace ran after his Daddy out the door and toward the car. Kenneth knelt down to pick him up.

"We get to take Mommy to the doctor," Kenneth told the toddler. "Call her. Say, 'Mommy, come on. Let's go.'"

"Mommy, go!" his little voice bellowed. Clella stuck the pin in her hat and grabbed her purse. She wasn't sure why they had to go. She knew what was wrong.

A short time later, they parked on Rolla Street in Hartville in front of Doc Lattimer's. Clella noticed a crowd gathered on the courthouse lawn under the budding magnolia trees.

"Oh, that's right. I had forgotten. Senator Reed is here campaigning for Franklin Roosevelt," Kenneth said.

"I don't need to hear anything. I'm voting for him," Clella admitted. "He's got to do better than Hoover." They went inside. It didn't take long for Doc Lattimer to confirm what Clella had already known. Their second child was on its way.

Doc Lattimer counseled her about her diet. "Be sure and drink plenty of milk. And how about meat?"

"We haven't had any in a while, but the hens are laying, and maybe we can get some pork from..."

"Well, even so, you're doing better than a lot," he said.

"We're thankful, I guess," Clella replied while buttoning her dress after the examination.

When Clella walked out of the exam room, she saw Kenneth, running his fingers through his hair, ignoring Wallace who was pulling on his hand. He stood as she approached. All she had to do was smile. Kenneth grinned and picked up Wallace. "Looks like you're going to be a big brother."

Chapter Twelve

This is the day which the Lord hath made; we
will rejoice and be glad in it.
......Psalm 118:24 KJV

October 25, 1932

In the living room, Kenneth stood up then sat back down. He watched two-year-old Wallace play with a basket of wooden thread spools in the middle of the cross-looped rug on the floor. Clella gasped and groaned from the bedroom. Hettie appeared in the doorway.

"Kenny, we need more hot water."

He heard her. He saw her lips moving, but his mind stalled.

"Kenny," she snapped.

"Right. Is everything okay?"

"Everything's fine," she said before returning to the room.

Kenneth went to the spring to fetch more buckets of water. "I should really see about digging a well," he mumbled.

***

Hettie pulled back the window curtain so her daughter could see outside from the bed. Clella knew her mother intended to help her relax and get her mind off the pain.

The autumn sun highlighted the oak and elm trees on the hill to the east of their cottage. October in the Ozarks was normally breathtaking, but today, Clella looked at dull colors which held more brown than usual, a countryside that had lost its luster. The drought of the past two summers drained the life out of everything. The air contained remnants of a dark haze left over by the most recent winds blowing in off the plains to the west. A severe drought plagued that whole middle section of the nation. Countless farmers lost their crops, and, in Oklahoma, their land was literally blowing away. The depression of the entire nation made food scarce and money practically nonexistent.

Another contraction gripped her body, and Clella gasped as she bore down.

Essie smiled and rubbed her forehead with a damp, cool rag while Clella labored to give birth to her second child. Essie and Jim were still without child.

The next pain came sooner and more intensely. Clella half gasped, half yelled.

***

As Kenneth carried a basin of water to the bedroom, he heard the faint cry of a newborn. Just like it had with Wallace, his heart twisted. Clella? Was she okay, or would this delivery take her from him forever?

Kenneth stepped inside the bedroom. Clella smiled as she reached to take their daughter from Hettie's arms. He moved closer. This precious little girl, like her brother, had thick, black hair. Kenneth kissed the warm, sweet baby and then bent to kiss his wife's forehead.

They named her Audrey Lee.

A few days later, after a meager evening meal of beans and cornbread, Clella tucked Wallace safely into bed, checked on the sleeping baby, and then sat with Kenneth to listen to the news on the radio.

"The country continues to suffer from what experts are calling a Great Depression," the reporter said. "Since 1929, ten thousand banks have failed, and over thirteen million Americans have lost their jobs. Many express dissatisfaction at the Hoover administration and its inability to take measures for economic recovery. Franklin D.

Roosevelt, the Democratic nominee, is favored to win in the upcoming election.

"In other news, the nation's Midwest and Southern Plains continue to languish from severe drought. Land that was once rich for crops and grazing now blows desolate as fourteen dust storms have been reported so far this year."

Clella glanced at Kenneth in disbelief. Clella thought maybe God was punishing the country for its sins. After all, even though the law prohibited people from making, selling, or consuming alcoholic beverages, the practices of all three continued. Greed and immoral behavior prevailed throughout the nation.

Along with most voters, Clella voted for Franklin Roosevelt who became the next president of the United States. In another glimmer of hope, Essie and Jim learned they, too, were to be proud parents. For Kenneth and Clella, that winter proved to be the most difficult yet. They had no money and a vanishing food supply.

Still, spring arrived and then summer.

One particularly hot summer night, Clella placed a tea towel over the plate of fried chicken and one over the mashed potatoes. Kenneth, who had taken a load of hay over to the Smiths, was more than two hours late for supper. The evening sun was setting behind the hills as Clella pushed the screen door open and walked out on the porch. The frogs croaked and crickets chirped. In the distance, she noticed a cloud of dust stirring up on the road. Surely this would be Kenneth. Her hopes faded as the dust path continued past their drive.

Where could he be? She had fed Wallace and Audrey an hour earlier and put them to bed. She knew Kenneth often lost track of time while talking. Still, what if something happened?

She sat in the rocker and watched for him. Darkness fell and little flashes of lights flickered as fireflies meandered here and there in the yard. Sitting there, she prayed he'd be all right. What would she do without him? It was unthinkable. He was probably the most stubborn man she'd ever known, but she loved him so much. Some nights when she would lay her head on his chest and listen to his heartbeat, she would thank God for every beat.

A light appeared in the distance up the hill and soon, she heard the familiar rumble of the truck. Relief swept over her. The truck turned in the drive much faster than normal and almost flipped over. It recklessly weaved from one side to the other as it continued the quarter-mile path up to the house before coming to a screeching, clanging halt. Kenneth opened the door and stumbled out.

"Hi, Clellie, baby!" he slurred as he tripped over the porch step. Clella gasped and reached out to catch him. He swung one arm around her neck and grabbed the post with the other. His breath reeked of alcohol. She opened the door and tried to help him inside.

"I bet you think I've been drinking," he said and burped, "but I haven't. I just had one little drink with Art." He placed his thumb and forefinger close together in illustration, "That's all."

Clella laughed, "Yes, I can tell you just had one itsy bitsy drink."

They stumbled into the bedroom and he fell on the bed, pulling her with him. Then he passed out. After she took his shoes and socks off and covered him, she went back into the kitchen to put away the uneaten food. It was a good meal, not one they could have every day. Kenneth knew when he left she expected him home to eat with his family.

She put the dishes away, clanging and clattering them on the shelves. She muttered, "Just *one little drink* my foot! He smelled like a distillery." She didn't like it, not one little bit. She stopped and took a deep breath. She couldn't help but feel thankful he was okay.

***

Every day, Clella walked down to the spring and drew water for drinking, cooking, and cleaning. It took three trips to the spring to draw enough water for cooking and bathing. Clella gave the kids baths every day. She filled the buckets and started back up the hill to the house. With each trip, they seemed heavier. In the summertime, she made these trips in the evenings because of the heat; in the wintertime, she usually made the trips in mid-afternoon. Each time as she returned, she swore the hill got steeper. Kenneth never offered to make this trip for her. Today on her third trip, she reached the house with buckets in hand only to find him smoking on the porch. Little Audrey, who had just learned to crawl, was crying inside while Wallace ran free in the yard. Her pulse raced with anger. She avoided looking at Kenneth, for fear she might say something she shouldn't. No doubt, he must think it was her duty alone to carry all the water.

"Wallace, come on," she called as she entered the side door into the kitchen. "It's time to wash up before bed."

That night as she laid her head on her pillow next to her husband, he reached out to caress her. Her back ached and her feet were swollen. She turned away from him. She hoped they would have a well and pump water into the house one day. Some people in town even had indoor toilets. That would be the most convenient, especially in winter when temperatures fell below freezing and snow covered the ground between the house and the outhouse. The depression made it hard to believe anything would ever be better.

The country experienced little improvement over the next few years.

For the Lathroms, the summer of 1936 brought only one heartbreaking change. Their dear Grandpa Frank went home to be with his beloved Susan in the presence of God.

Chapter Thirteen

How can a young man keep his way pure? By living according to your word.
......Psalm 119:9

Late February, 1937

"I don't know what else to do, Clella," Kenneth said as he took another sip of coffee while sitting at the kitchen table. Clella fried a skillet of eggs.

"Don't leave, Daddy," six-year-old Wallace pleaded.

"Be quiet, Dear. Your father and I are talking." Clella's concerned gaze locked with Kenneth's. As she scooped up eggs and put them on his plate, he caught her wrist.

"There's nothing else we can do."

"You're just going to leave me and the children, then?"

"Aubrey says the railroad work in Oregon is offering good pay, but I have to go now."

"You know I'm pregnant. How can you leave now?"

"I'll just work for two or three months, save up, and then I'll come back."

Nothing she said mattered. She couldn't stop him and maybe he was right. They had no money, practically no food and the dust bowl of the plains left a black haze even over their Ozark land. His plan was to hitch a ride with Artis, who was also going.

Clella packed Kenneth's clothes and prepared a bag of food for him to take. In the early morning, she stood on the sidewalk in front of Hattie's store, holding Audrey's and Wallace's hands as the car drove out of sight. A single tear spilled silently down her face. She was alone. She found it hard to believe he could so easily leave her knowing she was pregnant with their third child.

A month passed before she received a short note from Kenneth letting her know he arrived all right. *The work is hard, but the pay is good*, he wrote.

With the sharp edge of the hoe, Clella broke the dirt clods and prepared a small patch of ground to plant a few seeds for a garden– corn, green beans, watermelon, tomatoes, and peas. Every day as the baby inside her grew; she hauled water, chopped wood, and weeded the garden.

The mornings started early. Sometimes, Wallace milked the cow for her. Audrey gathered the few eggs. Even at four and six, they both did their chores. They had to because Mom needed them. At night, Clella cried herself to sleep as her back ached. Letters from Oregon arrived few, short, and far between.

Dear Clella, Wallace, and Audrey,
I'm fine. Working hard, but I like it. The men are all
hard-workers. It's beautiful here. I miss you.
Love,
Dad

He didn't ask how she was doing, didn't tell her he loved her, and wasn't even convincing about missing her or the children. She kept telling herself he was just working so much, but deep down, she figured he spent his free time drinking with his work buddies and flirting with the local girls.

She envied him. He might be working, but she remained at home with all the chores, tied down with two children and one on the way, while he must feel as free as a single man. She hoped he remembered that he belonged to her.

***

Kenneth wasn't used to hearing whistles, but since leaving home, he had become quite accustomed to them. He even welcomed the foreman's whistle, which signified an end to the workday. But, the most important one was the train's whistle when it arrived, carrying that week's payroll.

Kenneth woke before sunrise each day, and yet, that was still not as early as back on the farm. The rest of the day's events were a far cry from life at home. He missed his family. In plain view, he kept a picture of Clella, Wallace, and himself holding Audrey on the wall next to his bunk.

Before coming out west, Kenneth believed nothing could be prettier than his Missouri Ozarks, but they paled next to the giant redwood trees, which remained green all year round, and the rushing clear waterways full of trout and salmon. This Oregon country took his breath away.

As the foreman blew the whistle, everyone scurried around him. Kenneth jumped down off the pedal car and took the bandana from around his neck to wipe the dirt and sweat off his face. It was quitting time, but more than that, payday. Some of the men had families nearby, but most were like him—far away from home. All of them, however, shared a common bond. They were all just glad to have a job. Crowded around the foreman's stand, the workers waited for their names to be called to collect their earnings.

It seemed like it took the foreman forever to get to the "L's", but then he yelled out, "Latham?"

Kenneth stepped up. "It's Lathrom, Sir," he corrected, as he took his pay.

"Yeah, yeah. Matthews?"

Kenneth went back to the barracks to clean up. Afterward, he climbed in the back of a truck along with five others and headed to town and Lizzie's saloon. As they pulled up outside, he could hear music.

Lizzie's wasn't a small place, but when he entered, it was standing room only as he saw tables of men arm wrestling, others chugging beer at the bar, and someone playing the piano. About a half a dozen ladies served drinks. They wore short kick-up skirts and tied their hair with ribbon in curls that stacked on top of their heads. He stepped up to the bar and ordered a whiskey. At that moment, Kenneth was thankful Prohibition was over!

He took a drink and looked around the room. He recognized almost all the men from the railroad. Some were clean-shaven, some were scruffy and in tremendous need of a bath, but all of them were just happy to have a little bit of money to spend.

"Hey, Lathrom," his buddies yelled, and he nodded before heading over to their poker table. She caught his eye from across the room just as he sat down. With her painted red lips and long, black curls, she smiled in his direction. He removed his hat, which he would have done anyway, but he tipped it toward her before hanging it over the corner of the back of his chair. He was very much aware of her eyes on him as he played perhaps his best hands of poker ever.

> *Do not lust in your heart with her beauty or*
> *let her captivate you with her eyes.*
> *......Proverbs 6:25*

Chapter Fourteen

So do not fear, for I am with you; do not be
dismayed, for I am your God.
I will strengthen you and help you;
I will uphold you with my righteous right
hand.
......Isaiah 41:10

Wallace and Audrey ran on ahead of Clella, each carrying a bucket of water and sloshing some over the sides. Fortunately, the September air carried a slight chill. The children scaled the hill in front of her in no time and disappeared from sight. What Clella wouldn't give to have their energy! Instead, it was all she could do to put one foot in front of the other under the weight of the buckets she hauled. Being eight months pregnant didn't make things any easier. Once, she thought she might have to put one bucket down and come back for it, but that would make her off balance. She was almost there. She would make it.

When she saw the house, she noticed the strangest scene. Wallace and Audrey stood frozen, each still holding their buckets. They were about twelve feet from the front porch. What in the world?

"Wallace? Audrey? What's wrong?" Tears streamed down Audrey's cheeks, but neither she nor her brother uttered a sound or moved a muscle.

Then Clella saw it. Between the kids and next to the front porch, a huge copperhead snake was coiled up and poised to strike. The grayish-brown snake had a yellowish tail that wiggled slightly. It had a touch of orange on its head, and vertical eyes that stared at the kids. At the smallest twitch from either of them, it would certainly strike.

"Don't move," she told her children calmly, but there was nothing calm about the way she felt. She set her buckets down.

"Think, Clella, think. Help me, oh Lord," she whispered.

"Mommy's coming," she said evenly. She entered the house through the back door, grabbed the shotgun, and opened the drawer of the hutch. She fumbled trying to get shotgun shells. Her hands shook as she loaded the gun. She could see the kids through the front door. They didn't move an inch. She must kill the snake, *but what if I miss? What if it bites one of them? Copperheads are deadly. What if I can't get the children to the doctor in time? What if the doctor can't save them?* She thought frantically.

Clella quietly came out the front door onto the porch. She trembled, but knew she must steady herself. She had to do this. She couldn't miss, and it couldn't be allowed to strike.

She came from behind with the shotgun raised and took careful aim. With a loud bang, the shotgun blast severed the snake's head from its body.

Both Wallace and Audrey immediately started wailing. Clella set the gun down, ran, and took them into her arms.

"It's okay. There now. Momma got it. There's nothing to worry about," she crooned. She got them inside and took a cool rag and wiped their faces, still trying to calm them.

"I'm sorry, Mommy," Wallace said.

She lifted his chin. "What's there for you to be sorry about?"

"Daddy said I'm supposed to be the man of the house while he's gone, but I couldn't think of anything to do."

"Honey, you and Audrey did exactly what you were supposed to! You were perfectly still."

Wallace stood a little taller. "I told Audrey not to move," he said.

"Well, see. What a brave young man you are! You saved both of you."

He puffed up his chest.

"I couldn't move, Mommy. I was so scared," Audrey said, still shaking.

As Clella straightened, her back muscles cramped so much she felt weak in the knees and stumbled backward, leaning on the wall for support. She had to sit or lie down.

"Are you okay, Mommy?" Audrey asked.

"I'm fine," she lied while walking to a chair, hunched over and holding her belly. After she sat for a moment, she knew. "You know, I think Mommy's going to go lie down for a little while." She got up slowly and gingerly walked toward the bedroom. "Aunt Essie should be here in a little bit. Wallace, you watch for her, okay?"

"Okay, Mommy, but I don't want to go outside again, though."

"You don't have to, Honey. Just keep an eye out the window." She wanted them to have something to do. She needed to rest and get the pains to stop. They had made a plan for Essie to come every other day in the evening, now that it was closer to time for Clella to deliver.

Before the sun set, Wallace announced, "She's here," as he met his aunt at the door.

Essie brought Hettie Pauline and Dude with her. Essie named her daughter, who was ten months younger than Audrey, Hettie after her mom and Pauline, after Jim's.

"Mommy killed a snake, Aunt Essie," Wallace shouted, jumping up and down.

"She did?" Essie asked, glancing around the room.

Audrey leaned on the arm of the sofa, her face in front of Hettie Pauline's. "You should have seen it!" Audrey exclaimed.

Wallace bragged, "Yeah, it was probably thirty-feet long."

"That long, huh?" Essie asked, still searching the room. "Well..."

"Where is it?" asked Dude, heading to the door. "Can we see it?"

Wallace pointed. "It's out there in the yard, but I'm not going out there." he answered.

"Where's your mother?" Essie asked.

Audrey spoke up, "She's lying down. I don't think she feels well."

Essie didn't waste any time. She went straight to the bedroom where she found Clella resting flat on the bed. "Are you all right?" she asked.

"I'm hurting pretty bad. It's my low back." Essie sat on the edge of the bed.

"What happened?"

Clella told Essie about the snake. "I'm just trying to rest and get calmed down. But, it doesn't seem to be working."

"Should I go get the doc?"

"No, not yet."

"Of all the days for me to bring the kids," Essie sighed. "I brought Dude with me 'cause Mom isn't feeling well," she explained.

After Hettie finally relented and Delphie was sent to the sanitarium, Dude lived with Clella's parents. "I just thought they'd enjoy playing together."

"Well, I'm glad you did. They'll keep Wallace and Audrey distracted." Clella winced as pain shot through her back. She grabbed Essie's arm "I'm not having this baby before it's due, you hear me."

Essie removed Clella's hand and patted it. "Of course, you're not. Everything's going to be fine," she reassured her. "But, I don't think I'll be going anywhere. I'll get some dinner for the kids. You hungry?"

"No, I don't think so." Clella tried to control the pain. The baby wasn't due for another month. She grabbed her sister's arm once more. "Essie, why hasn't Kenneth come home?"

"I'm sure he has a good reason." Essie always gave people the benefit of a doubt. "How long since his last letter?"

Clella released her grip. "Around the first of August, about four weeks ago. He didn't say a word about when he thought he'd come home." Her voice took on an urgent tone as she changed the subject. "Oh, you know what? I left the buckets of water out by the shed. Would you mind bringing them in? And maybe Dude and Wallace can do the milking?"

"Don't worry. We'll take care of it. You just rest."

Clella cramped and continued having lower back pain, but rest she did. It wasn't like she had a choice. She silently prayed for the little life inside her. "Please, God, don't let the baby come before it's time."

Essie appeared at the door of the bedroom, drying her hands on the apron she had donned in the kitchen. "The boys are feeding the calves and doing the milking. And I got the water in. Honestly, Clella, I know the snake upset you, but you're probably hurting because of carrying those heavy buckets. I'm not sure why Kenneth hasn't dug a well."

"A well! That would be nice!" Jim and Essie had a well. In fact, they had to drill extra deep to reach water. It cost them, but Jim intended for them to have some modern convenience.

"Maybe when Kenny gets back, he'll have earned enough money to put one in," Essie said. "How are you feeling, now?"

"Some better."

"Well, I'm going to take the girls and go let Jim know what's going on. I'll leave the boys here with you and be right back."

"That'll be fine." Clella reached out and touched her sister's hand. "Thanks, Sis."

By the time Essie returned, the boys had finished the chores and night had fallen. Clella was sleeping, so Essie got the kids settled on pallets on the floor.

Chapter Fifteen

*All night long on my bed, I looked for the one
my heart loves; I looked for him, but did not
find him.
......Song of Solomon 3:1*

It had been almost nine months since Kenneth left. Clella didn't sleep at all the night before. His letter said he would be arriving on today's train. His original two to three months turned into what seemed a lifetime. She thought for sure he would've returned for the baby's birth. His letters seemed distant and devoid of the emotion she expected, the emotion she desperately needed. So many feelings swept over her, everything from excitement and anticipation to nervousness and anger.

Wallace pulled on his best pair of pants, which were a little short. Clella handed him a warm, freshly-ironed shirt. "Put this on," she told him, "and don't forget to comb your hair." Then she tied the sash of Audrey's dress into a bow before working on her hair.

"Ouch, Mom," her five-year-old daughter protested through the tangles.

"You want to look your very best for Daddy, don't you?" Clella pleaded.

Once the kids were ready, she donned the same old, but clean, grey wool coat she had worn for the past eight years and tied the belt tight around her once-again thin waist. She pinned a matching hat on her head. It was the slightest of head coverings with a splatter of netting. She bundled the baby in a quilt made patches of blue and pink pieced together from her old dresses and Kenneth's old shirts.

An hour later, Clella stood on the platform of the train depot at Mountain Grove along with Wallace, Audrey, and little four-week-old Linda Ellen. Together, they all waited for the eastbound train to arrive from Springfield and all points west. Clella cradled the baby in her left arm, while Audrey held tight to her other hand. Wallace stood beside them. They all anxiously watched the track as if the train might magically materialize and they would miss it. The November wind blew in occasional blasts of cold, but none of them seemed bothered by it. Though they hadn't yet caught sight of it, the train's whistle sounded in the distance. The railroad track ran east and west just south of the town square and curved around through the trees and out of sight past Lake Lilly.

Clella's hands began to shake along with her knees. Would she recognize her husband? What would she say to him after all this time? The whistle sounded again and the nose of the train rounded the curve. Wallace started jumping with excitement.

"Here it comes, Mommy!" he shouted. "Here comes Daddy!"

Audrey turned loose of Clella's hand and ran away jumping with excitement.

"Stay back out of the way," Clella warned, but she didn't have enough hands to grab them both.

The train slowed and the whistle blew almost continually as it crossed over Main Street. The shushing of the wheels on the track wound down. Finally, it came to a stop. The conductor, dressed in striped overalls and cap, stepped down from the train and placed a stool at the foot of the train's steps.

First, an older lady got off the train, but there was no sign of Kenneth. They waited for what seemed like forever. Clella saw movement in one of the windows. Kenneth walked through the door and turned toward the steps. He stopped, looked up, and for a brief moment, their eyes met. Before she could smile, his gaze fell to Wallace and Audrey, both of whom ran to meet him. Clella walked a little closer. Kenneth hugged Wallace and then picked up Audrey.

"Daddy, we missed you," Wallace said.

"I missed you, too."

Audrey spoke next. "Daddy, do you know what?"

"What?"

"We have a new baby!"

"Yes, we do!" He set Audrey down and came to Clella. Again their eyes met. She looked for something, anything that would convince her he still loved her. He bent to give her a fleeting kiss and she saw a difference in his eyes. She could feel it, too. It seemed like he avoided looking at her altogether.

Kenneth pulled the blanket back far enough to see his new baby girl. "Look at her, Mommy," he said. "It's been awhile since we had one this small, huh?"

"She's such a good baby," Clella said. "How was your trip?"

He took the baby from Clella and they all walked toward the car. "It was a good train ride. So much to see."

"Daddy, what's it like out west? What's it like in Oregon?" Wallace asked him.

"It's quite a sight, Son. The trees are so big and it doesn't get nearly as cold there in the winter or as hot in the summer. My, you've grown, Boy. How do you like school?"

"It's okay." Then he whispered, "Sometimes, Mom lets me sleep and she does the milking by herself."

"What about me, Daddy?" Audrey quizzed. "Don't you think I've grown?"

"Little girl, you've probably grown the most."

Clella smiled as she watched her husband with their children. It was good to have him home, but something wasn't right and she couldn't quite put her finger on it.

He talked easily with the kids, but why was he avoiding her? She needed that connection more than ever. She wanted to feel his strong arms around her, to know she was no longer alone.

"Daddy, Mommy killed a giant snake!" Wallace announced. "You should have seen her."

"Oh, yeah? Well, you know Mommy. She can do anything." He glanced at her and smiled. Once again, his gaze left her as quickly as it came.

Audrey's eyes widened. "Yeah, she shot it with the shotgun!"

***

That night, Kenneth blew out the lamp next to the bed and climbed in beside Clella. He rolled over and pulled her into his embrace. "It's good to be home," he told her.

She wished she could see him now. Search his face, his eyes, for any proof of what he claimed. "Is it?" she asked.

"Um, hum," he half groaned as he ran his hand over her body, stirring up familiar feelings. She gasped. It had been so long since she had felt his touch. Her body responded eagerly to his caress. Deep down, she knew something had changed, but what did it matter now? Maybe it was just the long separation. Maybe it was she. Maybe she resented his absence when she needed him most. She knew he had gone for the good of his family, to earn money so they could live. But just what price would they pay?

He touched her softly and kissed her, stirring the fire that was theirs alone to stoke and keep burning. He was home now. She had her husband back. He held her close and once again they became one.

***

The rooster crowed and the sun rose, as did the Lathrom household. Clella put a pot of coffee on the wood cook stove. Audrey hugged her mother in the kitchen.

"I'm so glad Daddy's home," she said.

Clella smiled, "Me, too." She saw Kenneth standing in the doorway, dressed in overalls, his mouth curved up in a smile.

"Come on, Audie, you can gather eggs while Wallace and I do the other chores and Mommy cooks breakfast." He handed Audrey her sweater, grabbed his coat and tipped his hat to Clella as they all walked out the door.

Clella started a skillet of sausage and another of potatoes and eggs. Linda had been awake at around 3 a.m., and it wouldn't be long until the baby would wake again. *Maybe I can make some biscuits this morning.* No sooner did she think that, the baby started crying.

Linda had just gone back to sleep when the gang returned for breakfast.

Clella set the table and began serving her family.

"I think we should buy dairy cows," Kenneth told Clella as she poured his morning coffee. Kenneth sat down and took a drink. "Yum, I missed that! I think we can make a little bit of money at it, what with the opening of Kraft Dairy."

"Maybe, but can we afford to buy the stock?" Clella had a better mind for business matters than her husband. If anyone knew whether they could afford it, she would.

"Well, surely, with the money I earned in Oregon we can make a start of it."

Clella sat down at the table opposite from him. "How much did you earn, Kenneth? You haven't exactly told me and you didn't send that much home."

"Well, enough to buy some cows," he snapped and rose suddenly leaving the table. "You let me worry about it." With that, he walked out the door.

Clella stared at her coffee. What was wrong with him? The baby stirred and half cried.

In a few short hours, life's routine took on a whole new normal. Kenneth left for town, and shortly thereafter, Wallace left for school. Only one thing remained unchanged– Clella stayed home alone with Audrey and the baby.

While Clella unpacked Kenneth's bag, she wondered about the change in him. She put away the socks and hung up his overalls. She found his shaving gear, and underneath those things, she found the dirty clothes. As she pulled them out, she smelled alcohol. There was another fragrance, like gardenias. She turned his dirty socks right side out. Then, like always, she checked the pockets of his dungarees and shirts for anything he might have left there that could be ruined in the wash. She found the pocketknife Grandpa Frank gave him when he was a boy. In the other pocket, she found a long, folded piece of paper. She slowly opened it to reveal his last pay stub. With this kind of money each payday, her husband would be correct. They should be able to afford a small herd! Something told her he hadn't made it home with that much.

As she gathered up all the clothes, she noticed something red on one of his shirts around the collar. There was that smell again. Was it like gardenias or lilacs mixed with the whiskey? Clella froze for a moment. Maybe she had just found the reason he seemed so distant. Who was she, this other woman? Was she the only one?

Clella sighed and piled the clothes with the rest of the wash she needed to do, since the baby's diapers needed attention. Of course, she would have to haul a lot of water up from the creek.

She turned and caught her reflection in the mirror above the dresser. She stopped to stare at herself. Her disheveled hair needed brushing. Sleep deprivation made her eyes puffy and dark. Her pale face was blotchy, and her lips were thin and colorless. The tattered old housecoat she wore needed cleaning from the sausage grease stains splattered on the front. She pushed her hair away from her face and pinched her cheeks. She turned sideways and back and placed her hands at her waist. The baby fat had almost completely disappeared and at least she had her figure. But how could she compete with someone she had never seen, someone she didn't even know?

Linda began to cry. She needed to be fed and changed, and life must go on. *Is this all there is?*

Mag left just this year for college in Springfield. Clella could've done that. She always did quite well with her studies. What if she hadn't married? What if she had decided to wait? Then, she, too, would have been as free as Kenneth may have felt the last few months.

Linda screamed, demanding attention again, and Clella bent over the cradle to pick her up. While the baby nursed, Kenneth returned home. He walked inside, stopped, and stared at his wife. Clella was intensely aware of his eyes fixed on her from the door. She had a blanket covering her and the baby. His mouth curved to one side in that familiar smile and Clella felt her face flush.

"What are you staring at?" she asked.

"You," he answered before walking over and pulling the blanket back gently to reveal little Linda suckling. "She is a precious little thing. And you, well," he looked her straight in the eyes, "you're beautiful." He bent and kissed her in a way that made her forget everything, the long separation, the lipstick, and the perfume. All that mattered now was she loved him and they were together at last.

"There's a farmer in Texas County that has some dairy cows for sale," he told her. "I'm going to make arrangements to pick some up this weekend."

"I think that's great!" she said.

"And the Cooper Company is offering to pay good money for staves to make barrels." Kenneth sounded pleased with his plans.

Chapter Sixteen

You will hear of wars and rumors of wars.
......Matthew 24:6a

September 1, 1939

The afternoon sun warmed Clella as she sat on the front porch, peeling peaches. Wallace, Audrey, and Hettie Pauline played tag in the yard while two-year-old Linda desperately tried to join in the game. Essie walked out the front door with a clean bowl and knife.

"I put those on low to cook," she said. The kids laughed and screamed as they ran and played while Clella and Essie sat peeling and slicing peach after peach.

"This is the last bushel," Clella told her. "Then we're done for the day."

"Mommy, what time is it?" Wallace yelled.

Clella looked at the clock just inside the door. "Five 'til three. Almost time for The Aldrich Family on the radio," she announced. The kids all cheered and ran inside.

Clella and Essie continued peeling and talking as the kids listened to their favorite show. The sound of "Henreeeeeee, Hen-ree Al-drich! Coming, Mother," could be heard as dramatic voices drifted from the square box on the table.

Then there was a beep, beep, beep, and the sound of typewriters typing. "This is a special news bulletin from Washington."

Essie and Clella both set their bowls down and went into the house. "It has been confirmed that Adolf Hitler and the Nazi Army have invaded Poland. This comes just one week after the two foreign ministers of the Soviet Union and Germany signed the Molotov-Ribbentrop Pact, which renounced warfare between the two countries of Russia and Germany. Thousands of Jewish and non-Jewish refugees fled into eastern Poland. Poland's allies, including the United Kingdom, Australia, and New Zealand, are expected to declare war on Germany. The entire globe is intensely watching this new development, which may indicate we are looking at what could be a world war of major impact. President Roosevelt is expected to address the union this evening. We will bring you more news as it becomes available."

Clella quickly turned the radio off. "You all go on outside and play some more before evening chores." Essie and Clella looked at each other. "What's going to happen next for heaven's sake?" Clella asked.

"Well, I've been saying they need to watch out for Hitler," Essie commented. "Jim and I think he's evil." James G., who was not yet four weeks old, awakened, crying. Essie went to get her infant son out of his cradle.

Clella stirred the peaches on the stove. She was checking on the pork roast she cooked for the evening meal, when Jim and Kenneth drove up outside. They all planned to eat dinner tonight and play some games afterward.

Kenneth walked through the door with Jim right behind him. "Daddy," Audrey said. "You missed 'The Aldrich Family'."

Linda ran to her daddy and he picked her up. "Oh, no. I can't believe I missed Henreeeee!"

Essie looked at Jim. "It was just on the radio. Hitler invaded Poland."

Jim gave her a look of incredulity. "They'd better watch him," he warned. Jim read everything he could get his hands on, so he and Essie knew more about foreign affairs than probably anyone around those parts.

Clella busied herself in the kitchen with dinner. They sent the kids outside to play, except for little Linda.

"Watch this," Kenneth told Jim. "Linda, where's your big toe?"

Not quite two years old, the toddler knew this drill well; she had performed it many times and appeared quite pleased to show off for the adults. Without looking, she pointed to her foot. "Tight dare," she said proudly. But not everyone laughed as they usually did.

"Where?" her daddy asked again.

She quickly looked down at her foot. In her haste, her finger had landed on her little toe instead. She quickly moved it to her big toe. "Tight dare," she corrected and they all roared.

In a few short minutes, the two families sat around the oak table in the Lathrom's kitchen enjoying pork roast, potatoes, gravy, and peaches and cream for dessert. They talked about this current news, the baby Kenneth and Clella were expecting in the spring, and the new teacher at Robinett School where the children would start soon. The adults tasked Wallace, Audrey, and Hettie Pauline with the evening chores while they all enjoyed a night of card games.

***

Autumn soon turned into winter. One cold night in January, the wind howled and caught the loose wood shingle on the side of the house, tapping it steadily against the window as what was sure to be Missouri's worst snowstorm of 1940 blew in. The door opened and cold burst through the house. Wallace carried in a bundle of firewood for the potbelly stove in the living room and Clella helped him push the door closed against the wind. Audrey worked on her homework and Linda carried her doll around, but both stayed close to the heat of the stove.

Night had fallen nearly three hours ago and Kenneth still wasn't home. This behavior had become normal for him. Earlier, he had taken a load of stave bolts to the nearby town of Manes, and more than likely, after he

- 97 -

received his pay, he had stopped off to have a beer or engage in a poker game. Clella was no fool. At least two women she knew were stalking her husband, vying for his attention. But at six months pregnant, she could do little about it. However, the dangerous condition of the roads gave her cause to worry.

"Mommy, it's so cold," Audrey said. Clella handed her a shawl and noticed Wallace starting out the door into the night again.

"Where are you going?" she asked. He pulled the collar of his coat up and put on his hat.

Ten years old and almost grown, she thought.

"One of the heifers is missing," he answered. "I'm going down to the creek bottom to see if she got stuck."

"I'd better go with you. This weather is pretty fierce." She pulled on her winter gear and put a scarf around her head. She turned to Audrey. "You stay here with Linda." Linda was two and a handful, but Clella knew she could manage. "Put your night clothes on and get ready for bed," she instructed, patting Audrey's head lovingly. She smiled as she looked at her precious daughters, one studious and growing much too quickly, the other still toddling and baby cute. "We'll be back soon."

Clella couldn't button her coat around her belly and the cold wind hit her face as she stepped outside with her son. She was proud of her family. Her eldest was growing into a fine, young man. Audrey was five years older than Linda, but she was the best big sister to a toddler who got into her homework, tore pages out of her book, and spilled milk on her new skirt. Clella ran her hand over her stomach. This new brother or sister would be here sometime in March.

The bitter cold blew through the heavy snow. As Clella and Wallace neared the creek and she stepped on a flat rock glazed with ice, her foot slipped. She flapped her arms wildly, trying to maintain balance despite her oversized belly. She gasped as her weight shifted and she fell backward. Just in time, Wallace braced her from behind with his steadying hands.

***

Audrey was happy to stay inside where it was warm, even if she had to look after her little sister. She started to dress for bed as her mother instructed, but it was so cold in the house and the stove was warm as long as she wasn't far away from it. She decided to sit back down for a little while longer. Linda started to cry so Audrey picked her up and held her in her lap. Both of them sat in front of the stove.

"Sshh," she softly told her little sister. "It's okay. Mommy'll be back soon." Audrey patted her head and sang, "Hush little baby, don't you cry..." Linda quieted down and rested her head against her sister's shoulder, but didn't close her eyes. Audrey rocked her back and forth and side to side. As she sang, the rhythm of the song slowed and she paused between words, before finally trailing off. The warm stove comforted her and the flickering candlelight was mesmerizing. Audrey, who had been up since before dawn, drifted off to sleep, holding her sister in her lap.

Suddenly, she woke to shrill screams. Linda was trapped on the floor in front of her between the rocking chair and the stove, her hands still pushed against its burning surface. Linda had apparently slipped and reached out to break her fall. Now, she couldn't move without pushing her hands against the hot stove. Audrey yanked her sister away from the searing hot surface.

"Oh, my God," she cried out. Linda screamed, writhing in pain. Audrey joined her wails, especially when she caught sight of her sister's bright red palms which already blistered.

***

As Clella and Wallace walked closer to the house, they heard the two girls screaming. Immediately, they began running, but the heavy snowfall and wind hindered their steps. Wallace broke ahead of Clella. She struggled with the additional weight of the baby she carried and the fifteen inches of snow she plunged into with each step. Still, she summoned a strength that was not her own. In her heart she prayed, "Please God, let my girls be all right."

Wallace burst through the door with Clella not far behind. They found the girls sitting in the middle of the floor still screaming. Audrey had her arms around Linda. When the toddler noticed her mother she held her hands up, wailing louder. Clella took one look at the blisters and knew the seriousness of the burns on her daughter's hands. She did the only thing she could think of. Quickly emptying the washbasin, she refilled it with coal oil. She grabbed her little one and held her hands fast in the liquid. Linda screamed even more. Audrey continued crying, and Wallace looked on in shock.

Tears streamed down Clella's cheeks. "I'm so sorry, Baby. It's going to be all right. It's going to be all right, now." Then she turned to Audrey. "It's going to be okay. Stop crying. Tell me what happened."

"I'm sorry, Mommy. I fell asleep. I didn't mean to." She started crying all over again.

"It's not your fault, Baby." Clella assured her.

"She fell and burned her hands on the stove," Audrey cried.

Clella glanced at Wallace and motioned for him to comfort Audrey while she tended to Linda. After she soaked Linda's hands, she covered them with lard and wrapped them in clean cloths.

"Now, now. It's okay," Wallace told Audrey while he gently hugged and rocked her. "It's not your fault. Everything's going to be all right." Audrey stopped crying, but she watched in horror as Linda continued to wail.

After some time, Wallace managed to get Audrey to bed, and he went to sleep, too. Linda eventually stopped crying, but she sniffed as her mother rocked her all night long.

Rocking in the dark, Clella wondered, *Where is Kenneth? He's always somewhere! Usually, somewhere else!*

At about two o'clock in the morning, Kenneth returned home. As he hung up his coat and hat, Clella watched him from the shadows. The moonlight reflecting off the winter snow through the windows created little patches of light inside the dark house. He turned and glimpsed her and Linda in the chair. Linda was sleeping, but he noticed the bandages on her hands.

"What happened?" he asked as he sat in the chair next to them.

Clella relayed the whole incident to him before asking, "What took you so long?"

"Oh, Baby. I stopped to play a little poker at Harvey's and the next thing, this awful storm came up. I got stuck down by Jug Rock Holler and thought I wasn't going to make it. I had to leave the truck and walk the rest of the way." He kissed her forehead. She smelled the alcohol. He warmed his hands over the stove and then offered to take Linda from her.

"No, you might wake her. She's been in such awful pain." Clella thought of many things she wanted to say to him, questions she wanted to ask, but if they argued, they might wake Linda and he always came up with an excuse. He sat silently beside her for a while before finally going to bed. Clella cradled Linda until sunup.

Linda cried and sniffled steadily for the next two weeks, and Audrey's eyes often brimmed over with tears looking at her. Clella dressed and bandaged Linda's hands three times a day. For the most part, Kenneth stayed home. Several times, he held his little one close to him.

While Clella took care of Linda, he and Wallace did the outside chores together. One evening when they came in for dinner, they kicked the snow off their boots and left them at the door. Clella cooked beans with ham and cornbread, while an almost healed two-year-old ran circles around her. She stood over the stove stirring the pot when Kenneth walked behind her, wrapped his arms around her pregnant belly, and kissed her neck. Her pulse quickened as he whispered, "I love you."

She smiled, placed her hand on his arm and leaned her head toward his. "Promise?" she asked, but their son interrupted the moment.

"Dad, can we turn on the radio?" Wallace asked.

Kenneth left his embrace and turned to answer, "After dinner."

Wallace and Audrey shouted with excitement and even Linda's face lit up some. Kenneth bent down and picked her up.

Later, they all sat in the living room and listened to "The Barn Dance" show on the radio. The baby kicked a lot as Clella churned butter while she watched her family laughing and dancing to the radio broadcast.

Chapter Seventeen

*I have told you these things, so that in me you
may have peace.
In this world you will have trouble. But take
heart! I have overcome the world.
.....John 16:33*

Sunday, December 7, 1941, started out like any
other December Sunday. Kenneth, Clella, Wallace, Audrey,
Linda, and twenty-month-old Wesley De, or Buck as they
called him, braved the bitter cold, loaded into their '36
Ford, and headed down the dirt road toward their country
church. They passed their neighbors' farms of snow-dusted
hills and crystal trees. America had just weathered the
worst economic decade in history and emerged as a
survivor. Rooster weathervanes sat atop freshly-painted red
barns, some of which even contained John Deere tractors.

Clella taught a children's Sunday School class.
Kenneth didn't always go to church. Truthfully, some
Sundays, he was just too busy with the farm, but Clella
knew it was also because he thought the folks judged him
for selling stave bolts used in making barrels for beer, wine,
and whiskey, among other things.

After church, they drove through Hartville. They
heard the church bells in town ringing. That wasn't normal.

"What do you think is going on?" Clella asked.

"Hey, Dad, the flags are all at half mast," Wallace
said. Audrey and Linda strained to see out the window.

Kenneth and Clella looked at each other.

"I wonder if something's happened to President
Roosevelt," Clella guessed.

Kenneth pulled the car over and parked on Main
Street. "I'm going to see what's going on," he said. He got

out and walked up to a crowd gathered on the corner. Clella watched as Clyde and Otis made dramatic gestures with their hands while relaying their news to Kenneth. *Whatever they're telling him must be shocking.* Kenneth shook his head, stomped his foot, and then stood with his mouth agape. They all talked for quite some time before he returned.

"What is it?" Clella anxiously asked.

His eyes wide with disbelief, he answered, "The Japanese have attacked Pearl Harbor. At least two ships have been sunk. President Roosevelt spoke to the nation over the airwaves just minutes ago."

"What does this mean? Why would the Japanese do such a thing?" It was more than Clella could comprehend. There had been much talk about Adolf Hitler, the war-ravaged countries he conquered, and air bombings over England, but it was hard to think about fighting on their own shores and with Japan.

"They took the Navy completely by surprise," Kenneth continued. "Who couldn't manage to counter much in defense."

"Oh, no, but I don't understand..."

***

They gathered that evening at Jim and Essie's, awaiting the presidential address from Washington, D.C.

"Well, for a country that chose to sit by and watch what's happening in Europe rather than fight against the atrocities of a man like Hitler, it looks like we'll be fighting anyway," Jim said. Audrey and Hettie Pauline ran through the house and into Hettie's bedroom, unmoved by national events.

Before any more could be said, President Roosevelt's voice sounded on the radio, and the four of them froze, hanging onto his every word. He spoke for some time, and elicited the most emotion when he said the

United States of America had declared war on Japan as a direct result of the attack on Pearl Harbor— an announcement that pleased almost all Americans.

Over the next few weeks, Clella read countless stories in the newspapers about recruitment lines filled with sons, husbands, and fathers ready to go fight for their country. Proud patriots filled boot camps. Clella knew several young men, and even some women, from the Hartville area who were ready and willing to put their lives on the line for God and country.

Journalists reported that the United States, which had been slow to enter the conflict with Hitler's Nazis, now became a major force in the global war. Just emerging from the effects of the Great Depression, the country utilized its economic, scientific, and industrial capabilities to serve the war effort.

The face of the country's homeland began to change. While America's men fought on foreign soil, the women took up the slack in the workforce. They filled all kinds of jobs once held by men, from factory jobs to sports competitions. Everyone did their part.

One spring afternoon, Clella and Essie took their children, hitched up the old wagon, and joined other citizens in Wright County for a scrap metal and rubber drive. Everyone was helping the war effort in one way or another. At the end of a hard day's work, they rested on a bench in front of the courthouse.

"Have you noticed Mother?" Essie asked Clella. "She doesn't look well."

"I hadn't thought about it." Clella took her eyes off the children playing on the lawn and turned to her sister. "What do you mean?"

"She's thinner and out of breath," Essie answered.

Now that Essie mentioned it, Clella did realize a difference in her mother. "You don't think that she's just getting older? You know she dotes on Dude. That's enough to wear anyone out."

"She has that cough." Essie sighed and yelled at James G. to get down from the tree he was climbing. "I'm concerned about her."

"Maybe Doc should take a look at her," Clella suggested. So, the two conspired to get their mother to the doctor.

**

Kenneth and Clella now had seventeen cows to milk. Most of the milking fell to Clella, Wallace, and Audrey because Kenneth drove the milk truck for the dairy. The mornings started early. Buckets of milk and milk cans were added to the other heavy items Clella carried, like the buckets of water she still hauled from the spring. A family of six required a lot of water for drinking, cooking, laundry, and bathing. Clella didn't like it, but she knew it had to be done. She enlisted the kids to share in what chores they could before they left for school.

Kenneth's milk route took all day and sometimes longer. Many times, Clella already had the kids bathed and in bed before he tore himself away from the poker game he joined after finishing his route. With America's troops searching for victory in Europe and on the high seas, Clella felt like she was losing a battle of her own–her marriage. Their lives were so different from those first days of love-filled aspirations. Her back ached, and by evening, exhaustion overtook her.

Clella put Kenneth's supper in the ice box and blew out the lamp in the kitchen. When she turned around, she found Wallace standing in the doorway.

"You don't suppose Daddy had to give Colleen Dawson a ride again, do you?"

"What do you mean 'again'?" she asked.

"I heard him telling Otis that she waits for him on his route and he gives her a ride."

Clella's heart raced as she stared at her son. "Is that so? Did he say anything else?"

"No. Nothing that I heard."

"I'm sure he'll be home soon." She placed her hands on Wallace's shoulders and turned him around. "You go on to bed now, Son."

Once he'd gone, she leaned against the cupboard, her eyes roaming to and fro as she tried to comprehend the meaning of what she'd just learned. This information from her twelve-year-old son just set her world reeling. Colleen Dawson was divorced. She always wore her clothes a little too form-fitting. Her ruby red lips came out of a tube, and her cheeks blushed unnaturally. Colleen flirted shamelessly with men at close range. She had no business hitching a ride with Kenneth. He belonged to Clella.

Clella sat up and waited for him in the dark. Thinking about their life together, she knew things hadn't been the same since Kenneth returned from Oregon. Sometimes she thought something was wrong with her, but deep down, she knew her husband had changed. He didn't care that she worked so hard. Nor did he pay her the attention he had in the past.

***

Kenneth quietly opened and shut the door. He softly hung his hat on the hook and crept toward the bedroom when he noticed her silhouette.

"You're getting in kind of late, aren't you?" she asked.

"Awe, I stopped and had a cold one with the boys."

"Play any poker?" Her tone was calm and even.

"Yeah, a little."

"Did ya give Colleen a ride today?"

He sat down in the chair opposite her. "What are you talking about?"

"Don't act like I don't know. I do." He hung his head. She lit the lamp on the table because she wanted to see him more clearly. "You've been giving her rides to town and no telling what else." She paused. He didn't move or say a word. Then she raised her voice, "What else, Kenneth?"

"Clella, it's not like I want to. She waits for me. What can I do? Tell her no?"

"Yes. That's exactly what you should do. People will be talking. Even our son knows."

He stood up defiantly. "You're always worrying about what people think. This is silly. Colleen needs a ride from time to time and I'm going that way anyway. It doesn't mean anything."

"It means something to me." She stood in front of him.

He put his arm around her and pulled her close to him. "Why? Are you jealous?" His mouth curved in that slight smile and his eyes twinkled. His breath smelled faintly of alcohol. Why should she be jealous? After all, she was his wife. She hated that he had made her question him.

"You know I'll always love you, Mama." His arms closed around her. She searched his face for the truth. Yes, it was there. She saw the love she longed for in his eyes. A love she hadn't seen in a very long time. What was it that Colleen saw when she looked into his eyes? Was it just lust? Was it adventure? It couldn't be love. Then, he tenderly bent and kissed her and she warmed with excitement. As they walked arm-in-arm to the bedroom, all thoughts of "what's her name" completely vanished. Tonight, he belonged to her.

***

On the war front, the Western allies invaded Sicily in 1943 and initiated several operations against Japan in the Pacific. America gained little victories at a great cost of life, and, at this point, no one was certain of the outcome. A bitter struggle still ensued in Europe between the allied forces and Hitler's Nazis.

On the home front, 1943 brought Kenneth and Clella their fifth child, a little girl named LouAnn. Kenneth no longer feared for Clella in childbirth. But perhaps, he should've been more concerned this time. At a birth weight of almost ten pounds, LouAnn's difficult delivery took almost twenty four hours. Hettie remained at her side, but it became apparent she wasn't well. Many times, she stopped and leaned against the doorframe.

LouAnn was the last grandchild Hettie helped deliver. The next year, Grandma Garner's grave illness became evident. It would, however, be Grandpa Lathrom who passed into eternity first. Kenneth and his father had grown close in the last few years. He remained sad, quiet and withdrawn for weeks, crying upon anything that reminded him of De.

The Garner girls shared in caring for their dying mother. They would have had it no other way because Hettie had always cared for them. Unfortunately, this pulled Clella away from her own home.

"Mama," Clella said as she wrung out the washrag in the basin and gently cooled her mother's forehead. "It's me, Clella."

Hettie, now a mere skeleton of the woman she had been, didn't open her eyes. When Clella picked up her mother's hand, Hettie managed to squeeze hers slightly. Her mother suffered much over many months before finally succumbing to the illness. Clella's heart broke.

After Grandma Garner passed, Dude went to live with Clella's family. Dude and Wallace, both at fourteen, got along well, but the Lathroms needed a bigger home. The "Montie Place", located south of Highway 38 and not far from the Lawson School, was for sale. That nice piece of land had a springhouse, but no electricity or well and definitely no running water to the house. They purchased it and began working the land. Wallace and Dude could help, but at four-and-a-half years old, Buck wasn't yet old enough.

Clella still had to trek down to the spring to fetch buckets of water for her family's needs. Of course, Kenneth drove the milk truck and the family helped, doing everything from milking the cows to cleaning the milk cans. They even cleaned the cans of others on the route who failed to adequately do so. Their dairy farm was doing quite well.

As life on the farm continued, the country continued battle on the warfront. Most Americans didn't know the federal government secretly worked on a highly dangerous weapon until after it was deployed. American scientists hoped it would ensure the preservation of the United States and bring an end to the war. In the summer of 1945, President Truman made the fateful decision to drop this atomic bomb on Hiroshima and Nagasaki, Japan. The unleashing of this nuclear weapon sacrificed the lives of many Japanese men, women, and children, but Clella believed the president would not have acted thusly unless he thought it was absolutely necessary. The Japanese surrendered, and with Germany's earlier defeat and Hitler's suicide, U.S. troops headed for home. All of America celebrated.

Life on the Lathroms' Ozark farm was hard, but while the country listened to the big band sounds of Benny Goodman and the Dorsey Brothers, Kenneth and Clella kicked up their heels square-dancing with many of their friends to the sounds of a bluegrass mix of country. One evening in the fall of 1945, it was the Lathroms' turn to host a dance. Wallace, Dude, and the whole family worked together to carry all the living room furniture out onto the lawn to clear room for a dance floor, as was the custom. Johnny Smith, a local caller, called while the Moonlighters fiddled and strummed the peppy tunes of the Ozark Hills.

Clella and Kenneth made quite a couple on the dance floor. They laughed and enjoyed each other. How wonderful it was to take a break from the burdensome chores of their everyday lives. In this kind of diversion, Clella almost found the man she loved once more.

The Moonlighters were scheduled to play in the town square in Mountain Grove the following Saturday. When the day arrived, Clella woke early, and after she fed her family breakfast, she combed three-year-old LouAnn's beautiful, thick black curls while the rest of the family finished their chores. Then Clella gathered all the children into the car and Kenneth drove them into town to buy groceries. Each week, they either went to Hartville or Mountain Grove to get supplies and visit with friends.

Kenneth parked on the square in Mountain Grove. "Mom, I see Ruth," Audrey said as the children got out of the car. "Can I go with her to buy a soda at the fountain?"

"Yes, go on." Clella watched as Audrey ran across the grass to where Ruth waited. Glancing toward the gazebo, she smiled when she saw Wallace, Dude, and their friend, J.C., talking to the Claymore sisters.

Linda and Buck fought over a licorice stick. "Mommy, Buck took my candy stick," Linda complained.

"Did not," he argued. "It's mine." But then, Linda grabbed it out of his hand and he subsequently pulled her hair.

Clella grabbed him by the arm. "You two'd better behave or I'll get a switch. You both come with me to buy groceries." Clella could barely hold LouAnn's hand and keep Buck corralled with the other. Just before they went inside the store, she stopped and noticed Kenneth tipping his hat in the distance. His lips moved, and she knew he'd just uttered, "How do," to Eva Hicks, who laughed and said something before flinging her hair back over her shoulder. He laughed too, and watched as she walked away from him. Clella fumed.

"Hi, Mrs. Jones," Buck said as a woman they all knew walked out of the store. "You're looking really pretty today," her six-year-old son flirted. Clella's eyes widened as she looked at her son with astonishment, though she wasn't sure why. Since Buck started talking, he could charm the socks off a rattlesnake, if a rattlesnake had socks, of course. His cute smile and sparkling eyes lit up upon demand, and he never knew a stranger.

"Why thank you, Buck," the lady answered. She and Clella laughed briefly. Clella turned to her son and commanded him to go join his father.

Later, before the sun went down, Kenneth and Clella joined their neighbors in front of the gazebo to listen to the Moonlighters play. The kids talked and played tag with their friends.

That fall, Audrey and Hettie Pauline attended eighth grade at Lawson School along with many of their younger siblings and cousins; Aunt Ola was their teacher. Luckily for the Lathrom kids, the school was just around the corner and down the hill from their farm. Instead of a one-room school, it actually had two rooms, and first through eighth grades attended there. During the afternoons, Ola read to the class a book titled *Little House in the Big Woods,* written by a local author, Laura Ingalls Wilder. Clella enjoyed hearing about it from the kids when they returned home after school.

Chapter Eighteen

*To the Lord I cry aloud, and he answers me
from His holy hill.
.....Psalm 3:4*

December 5, 1946

It was a fair day for December, but the dark clouds of a cold front slowly rolled in. Clella sped into town, and the tires screeched as the car came to a sudden stop outside Doc Mott's office. She threw the door wide open, grabbed the bundle in the seat next to her, and ran into the doctor's office. Her heart beat wildly. She raced on past those waiting and flung open the door to the doctor's exam room. Doc Mott was listening through his stethoscope to little five-year-old Dolly Lawson's chest as she sat cooperatively on the exam table.

With tears in her eyes, Clella screamed, "He's not breathing! He's been gasping for air and now he's blue!"

Doc Mott immediately took Clella's newest son, Larry, from her arms and laid him gently on the exam table as Nurse Anna helped Dolly down and out of the room. Larry was barely three weeks old and, by his bluish tint, had apparently given up the very difficult task of breathing through restricted airways. Doc Mott moved quickly to administer a drug and some kind of vapor. Clella wrung her hands as tears continued to stream down her cheeks. Doc Mott glanced at her and said, "Hang in there, Mother. He's not gone."

She gasped and started to pray silently just as she had been doing in the car all the way into town. *Oh, God, please let him breath.* She never wanted to hear a baby cry so badly in her life. She watched as the doctor worked on her tiny baby boy. Eventually, he began to breath deeper and deeper. His skin gradually pinked up. Clella suddenly collapsed into a chair.

"You okay?" Doc asked her.

She nodded. "I thought he was dead," she softly cried.

"It's called asthma," Doc Mott explained. "The bronchial tubes swell, and breathing becomes harder."

"How serious is this?" Clella asked.

"Well, it can be very serious. I'm going to give you some medicine to give him whenever he has an attack. He's small, so you'll have to be careful to give him the correct dose." Larry's tiny little hand gripped Clella's finger as she watched him revive. She laughed through tears. How thankful she was to know he would be all right.

Relieved, she walked out of the doctor's office with Larry in her arms and climbed into the car. As she started the automobile, she saw Kenneth's milk truck pulling into the town square.

Good, she thought. *I need to go tell him about Larry.*

His truck stopped, and he jumped out and ran around to the passenger side. Clella froze as Colleen Dawson stepped down, dressed in a flattering black dress with a low neckline, revealing a shameful amount of cleavage. Colleen laughed and leaned closer to Kenneth while he held her hand. He laughed, too, paying Colleen his complete attention. Clella suddenly felt an overwhelming exhaustion. She watched Kenneth get back in the truck and drive on. She, too, put the car in gear, turned it around, and started back home, stunned and quiet.

Kenneth still hadn't returned home by the time Clella tucked the last of her children in bed that night.

"Momma, is Larry going to be okay?" Linda asked when Clella kissed LouAnn and pulled the covers up over her.

"Oh, Honey, he's going to be just fine," she assured her.

Clella checked on baby Larry in the crib next to her before she blew out the lamp and climbed in between the covers of her empty bed. She lay there and thought about the events of the day. Wallace, Dude, and Buck were asleep in their room. Audrey, Linda, and LouAnn slept in the other room. And Kenneth, she could only assume, must be captivated by a most engaging game of poker and drinking with the guys. Or maybe he was somewhere else altogether. *At any rate*, she thought, *the sun will rise tomorrow and there will be cows to milk, cattle to feed, eggs to gather, hogs to slop, breakfast to cook, dishes to clean, laundry to wash, butter to churn, water to haul, and more.* Clella thought about her life. How did she end up here? Tears moistened her face and fell onto her pillow.

Life goes on, she thought, *and I must get some sleep.*

***

Spring 1948

Each morning, Wallace, Dude, and Audrey caught the bus for Mountain Grove High School. They woke up at 4:30 in order to get their chores done, including milking nineteen cows, before the bus got there. Linda and Buck shared in these chores, too, before walking to school.

This morning, Allie Oliver's school bus stopped for Wallace, Audrey, and Dude, and they climbed on board. The bus would take them to the high school. Wallace, who had become quite the football star for the Mountain Grove High Panthers, wore his much-coveted letter jacket. He smiled at Betty Lou as he sat next to her.

As Audrey sat next to Hettie Pauline, her eyes caught the very stylish purple-plaid skirt and blouse worn by Helen Massey who sat right across the aisle. Audrey's eyes widened slightly as she saw the pennies tucked neatly beneath leather flaps on the tops of Helen's shiny, polished brown loafers. Helen looked really sharp.

"Hi, Helen, I like your shoes," Audrey said.

"Oh, thanks. My mom and I bought them at Brown's shoe store in Mountain Grove," Helen answered, elevating her nose slightly as she talked. "It's too bad you only get to buy one pair of shoes a year. These are the latest fashion."

Audrey ignored her stinging words and turned to talk to Hettie Pauline.

"Never mind her," Hettie Pauline said. "Did you get your English assignment done?"

They talked as the bus rolled along the winding country road on its way to school.

That evening, the Lathroms gathered around their big, round oak table for dinner.

"What did her dress look like?" Clella asked after Audrey told her about Helen and the penny loafers.

Linda and Buck started scuffling. "Stop that you two. Not at the dinner table," Kenneth scolded.

"It was a purple plaid and it wasn't really a dress. It was like a skirt and blouse."

"Oh, that does sound pretty." Clella dished up mashed potatoes for LouAnn and passed the bowl to Wallace.

"Yes, and the skirt was pleated. It looked really cute. It's the latest fashion," Audrey said as she ate a forkful of mashed potatoes and gravy.

Clella cut up LouAnn's roast beef before she started eating her own.

"Daddy, do you think we could buy a pair of penny loafers for me?" Audrey asked.

"Pennies!" Kenneth replied. "Why does one need pennies in one's shoes?" he asked and looked at Clella.

"Oh, Daddy, please?"

"There's nothing wrong with the shoes you have. It's not time to buy new ones," he answered. He was right.

Just as Helen had said, the Lathrom kids bought only one pair of shoes a year, and that wouldn't happen again until next fall.

One day the following week, when Audrey came home from school, she went straight to her room and put her books down. Clella leaned against the door post and watched her. Earlier that day, Clella had laid out a pleated skirt of blue and black and styled with little glass buttons. Audrey gasped and gently caressed the familiar material.

"Like it?" Clella asked.

"Like it? Oh, Momma, you made it from your own dress and you made a matching vest, too." She ran and gave her mother a hug. "I love it. Can I try it on?"

"You'd better."

Looking in the mirror, Audrey exclaimed, "It does fit and looks even sharper than Helen's store-bought one." Clella smiled. She had sewn each stitch with love for her oldest daughter.

The next Saturday, when the family went to Mountain Grove to buy their goods, Clella pulled Audrey aside and they went into the shoe store on the square. With the grocery and egg money Clella had saved here and there, she purchased a pair of shiny new penny loafers.

Audrey was a beautiful girl and it was her first year in high school. After all, what was a mother to do?

***

Sitting at the kitchen table, Kenneth raised his voice. "Clella, why are you so against this?" he argued. "He doesn't like school. And he's a big help here on the farm."

"Mother would've wanted Dude to finish school and we should encourage him."

"If he's not happy, it isn't going to do him any good anyway," Kenneth argued.

Though Kenneth and Clella disagreed on many things, they never argued much. Perhaps, repressed feelings over other matters fueled the exchange over Dude tonight.

"He wants to work with his hands, Clella, instead of being cooped up in some classroom with some really bratty kids," Kenneth reasoned. "I can use him here on the farm."

Clella stopped drying the knife she held in her hand and stared at him. "You spend more time with Dude than you do with your own son." It was true. Kenneth and Dude always hung out, either baling hay or drinking whiskey together.

Just then, Linda and LouAnn came frantically running up to the house.

"Mommy, Daddy, come quick," they screamed. "Buck's dead. He turned the tractor over down at the creek." Linda and LouAnn both struggled to catch their breath.

Clella's heart skipped a beat and she glanced at Kenneth. She dropped the butter knife and the two of them darted out of the house, running with the girls. Clella saw the empty spot in the field where the tractor had been parked. Tractor accidents were not uncommon and could very easily claim a life. They ran all the way to the creek.

Clella wouldn't allow herself to believe the worst. Buck had to be okay. Their fourth child had inherited his Dad's smile and that same twinkle in his eye. Even though he usually got into mischief, his outgoing personality and charm made him a favorite with adults and children alike.

With the creek now in sight, Clella gasped. She saw their tractor upside down in the gulley. She was afraid to look, afraid of what she would see, but she pressed onward, her heart pounding in her throat.

Kenneth and Clella searched the site of the accident, to the left of the tractor, to the right, underneath the wreckage, fearing Buck might be trapped there, but there was no sign of him anywhere.

LouAnn yelled, "There he is." She pointed up the hill.

With his knees drawn up to his chest, there sat Buck, mumbling. "What am I going to tell them?" he whispered over and over. The blood covering his face dripped onto his pants. He hadn't noticed them and appeared to be in shock.

Relief swept over Clella as tears threatened. "Buck!" Clella gasped, sprinting up the hill to him. At this he looked up and jerked at the sight of her and Kenneth.

"Are you all right? Where are you hurt?" She asked, turning his head one way then the other. He had a gash across his cheek, which looked fairly deep. Besides that, he escaped with only scrapes and bruises.

"I'm fine, but..." he looked at his dad, "I'm sorry, Dad."

"Son, haven't I told you to stay off that tractor?" Kenneth yelled. "Now I have to figure out how I'm going to get it fixed!" Kenneth was furious.

Linda turned to LouAnn and whispered, "I bet Buck's gonna get it when we get home!"

"Let's get you back to the house so I can tend to those wounds." Clella wrapped her arm around him.

For years, the family would laugh about this incident. Buck would never live it down.

Chapter Nineteen

*Husbands love your wives, just as Christ loved
the church and gave himself up for her.
......Ephesians 5:25*

Despite the objections of most of the members of the Garner family, Dude withdrew from school. While Dude and Kenneth spent long hours working together, Wallace graduated from Mountain Grove High School.

***

One morning, in the early fall of 1949, while Clella washed the dishes, Essie frantically rushed into the house.

"Essie, what is it?" Clella asked while drying her hands on the dishtowel.

"Jim's in the hospital in Springfield."

"Why? What's happened?" Clella hugged her sister.

"Doc Mott's not sure what's wrong with him." Essie started to cry, "but said he needed to get to the hospital. They took him right then. I have to go. Can you take me to the train station?"

"We'll go right now. James G. and Hettie Pauline can stay here after school. You don't worry about a thing." Clella soon had Larry and Essie in the car.

In the days that ensued, they learned Jim had contracted spinal meningitis and his condition was grave. He fought for his life as most cases like his resulted in death.

The family faithfully prayed for his healing daily. For eight months, Essie visited her husband almost every day. Many of those days Kenneth dropped her at the bus depot and picked her up later. Gradually, Jim's condition improved.

For Audrey and Hettie Pauline's graduation in 1950, the hospital conditionally released Jim to go to the baccalaureate service, but only if he agreed to return to the hospital immediately thereafter. One week later, he got to return home for good.

Audrey and Hettie Pauline started college in Springfield, Missouri, but Audrey loved Alan Oliver, her high school sweetheart, who worked in Peoria, Illinois. That Thanksgiving, they married. Alan worked for Caterpillar, a farm equipment manufacturing company that also hired Audrey as a secretary. Wallace started working there, too.

About that time, however, Uncle Sam drafted young men to serve in the Korean War, and Wallace was no exception. Whatever his future plans were, he would have to put them on hold until he returned.

Kenneth, Clella, and Audrey went to his graduation from boot camp at Fort Leonard Wood. The four of them had a picnic in the woods and took pictures. In one, Wallace and his sister stood side by side, arms wrapped around each other. Wallace took a picture of his parents sitting on the back of their car. Just before he snapped the picture, Kenneth put his arm around Clella and whispered a joke in her ear. It made her laugh. They all enjoyed the day, but it was soon time to say their goodbyes. Audrey hugged her brother, and Kenneth, his son, and though Clella tried not to, she cried.

During Wallace's tour in Korea, she wrote him every day.

Just as the Industrial Revolution rapidly changed American culture, Kenneth and Clella's lives meta-morphosed into a different season. Caterpillar grew rapidly, making combines for harvesting and other heavy equipment used in all types of construction. The Midwest began to prosper. When Wallace returned from Korea, Caterpillar took him back. Alan eventually talked Kenneth into applying for a job there, too. When they offered him the job, it was a great opportunity to make good money, but it was over four hundred miles away.

"I just think I should go first and then I'll send for you," Kenneth told Clella. To her, it sounded a lot like that fateful conversation they had years ago before he went to Oregon. Somehow, she didn't care anymore. She wanted him to love her as he once did, but their lives had evolved into something different.

This time, however, he returned, sold the livestock, and took her and their four youngest children with him. Alan and Audrey had a nice home in Marquette Heights. They all moved in together, and the Lathrom children enrolled in school. Larry started first grade. Clella cared for Alan and Audrey's baby, Al, her firstborn grandson, while the children attended school and the adults worked.

Life in Peoria was quite different. It was the early 1950s and they lived in a suburb with paved streets and quaint little homes. There was no need to carry buckets of water because the water came straight out of the faucet. The basement had an automatic washer and dryer in the laundry room. The gas cook stove took some getting used to and the furnace provided heat in the wintertime.

All these amenities eliminated several chores to which Clella was accustomed. She no longer hauled water or scrubbed clothes. She didn't have to carry in wood for the cook stove or the wood-burning stove, nor did she have the burdensome task of cleaning out the ashes, and there were no more late night walks to the outhouse in the wintery cold.

Her grandson was the best little baby, and taking care of him was like a dream. Of course, that may have been attributable to the new modern conveniences in her life. Clella thanked God for her blessings, perhaps experiencing a temporary false sense of happiness.

Here in Marquette Heights, American suburbia, life was grand. She prepared Kenneth's lunch box, including a thermos of coffee, and he left for work each morning. The bus picked up the kids and dropped them off after school. Each evening, Clella cooked dinner for the whole gang when they returned at the end of a full day's work. Their schedules were all the same, at least in the beginning.

Wallace roomed with J.C. Watts and drove a Harley Davidson. Kenneth began spending a lot of time with Wallace and his friends. At first, Clella was pleased. She was happy her husband was building a better relationship with their son. However, after some time, it became apparent Kenneth preferred spending his time with the younger men and ladies. They hung out at the bars and nightspots.

After twenty-three years, Clella became acutely aware of the changes in her marriage, like changing leaves through the seasons of a year.

"Where's Kenneth?" she asked one evening when he didn't come home with Audrey and Alan.

"He went with Wallace and J.C., I think, to play pool," Audrey answered before picking up baby Al to change his diaper.

Buck sacked groceries at a little store around the corner. Linda listened to rock 'n' roll records with Dot, a friend from school. LouAnn sat at the kitchen table, doing her homework.

Clella, once again, kept the food warm as best she could for her husband. Later that evening, she drove Linda around the subdivision so she could sell Christmas cards to earn money for the holidays. She picked Buck up from work. She helped LouAnn with her homework, and made sure LouAnn and Larry bathed before bed. Just before getting all the kids tucked in, she saw the headlights and heard the car pull in the driveway. Her husband was finally home.

Kenneth walked in the front door just as she picked up the pans, which held his dinner, and purposefully, stomped past him.

"Want dinner?" she asked defiantly as she opened the front door. Dumfounded, he stared at her. With a swift motion, she tossed the food out on the lawn. "There it is. Go get it."

She walked back into the kitchen, tossed the pans in the sink, and immediately went to bed. He didn't follow her, nor did she want him to. The kids observed her unusual behavior from their bedroom door.

"Get back in bed," their dad told them. Audrey was with the baby, and Alan sat in the living room with his father-in-law as Clella sought the solace of sleep.

This was the beginning of the end. Or maybe it actually was a progression that began many years ago on that spring morning when she waved goodbye and watched her husband drive away to the west.

Maybe this happens to couples who fail to communicate or care about one another, who go separate directions each day and fail to come back together again in the haven of their bedroom, which should be their "secret garden," Clella thought. *Perhaps work and the stress of life harden them to a point of numbness. Their hearts ache and their partners are clueless about why, or how to respond, or even if they want to. They begin to make mistakes that have lifelong consequences.* Deep down, Clella knew she and Kenneth were headed down such a path.

Audrey and Alan were expecting again, with the baby due in July 1953. The house wasn't big enough for all of them. Kenneth and Clella started looking for houses. On the weekends, they drove through the city and looked at homes for sale. They looked in Marquette Heights, Washington, and Peoria. Clella wasn't difficult to please, any one of them would do. Each time they toured a house, she got excited at the patio, or the modern kitchen, or the size of the basement, or the number of bedrooms. She pictured her family living the modern suburban life–a home with a picket fence, a television in the living room, and a radio in the kitchen.

"We can't afford this one," Kenneth said and walked away from her toward the car.

She turned and followed him. "Yes, we can. You're making good money at Caterpillar." Clella knew very well they could afford any of the houses they toured. She only chose the ones within their price bracket.

"No, the payments will be too high."

"Kenneth, they won't either." Clella was much better at arithmetic than her husband. She knew how much the payments would be and she knew they could afford it.

"Clella, we can't do it. That's all there is to it." He wouldn't look at her.

"Then what are we going to do?" she asked wrinkling her forehead and shrugging her shoulders in confusion.

"Well, I don't know. We still have the farm."

She lifted her eyebrows. *What does he mean? What's he saying?*

"Kenneth, our life is here, now. We can sell the farm."

"We're not going to sell the farm!" he raised his voice. They closed the car doors and he backed out of the driveway of a beautiful modest home complete with picket fence.

"We can afford both for a while," she reasoned.

"Why are you always nagging me?" he shouted at her. "We just can't buy a house right now, Clella, even though you want one."

"Then what is it *you* want to do, Kenneth?" There was silence. He looked only at the road straight ahead. Her heart raced wildly. She shook her head when he finally answered.

"I think until we have more money saved, you and the kids should move back on the farm, and I can move in with Wallace."

"That's what you want," she whispered. The car turned into the driveway of the house they had called home for almost a year. Kenneth turned the key and silenced the motor. They sat in the car without moving. Finally, Clella added, "You want to be free of me. That's what you want, isn't it?"

He didn't deny it, and he didn't reach out and touch her hand. "It's just that I think it makes the most sense," he replied.

"It makes the most sense? It makes the most sense?" She shouted. "There's nothing sensible about you not living with your wife and family. Buck and Linda, they need their father. Their life is here. They like the school. LouAnn is a whiz in her math class and Larry's been healthier here than he was all of his first years in Missouri." She opened the car door, and then turned back angrily, "And if we don't have the money, it's because you're too busy drinking with your buddies and losing it playing cards." She slammed the door and ran into the house, heading straight to her bedroom.

She knew things hadn't been right between them. He hardly ever spent any time with her or the kids. Instead, he ran around drinking and playing with a younger crowd. She had bided her time, hoping he was going through a phase, like a mid-life thing, but truthfully, he was breaking her heart. She cried herself to sleep that night and her stomach ached. Perhaps there was someone else. Maybe he had fallen in love with someone else. He didn't seem to love her anymore.

Chapter Twenty

*She considers a field and buys it; out of her
earnings she plants a vineyard.
......Proverbs 31:16*

The green pasture waved as a gentle August breeze
stirred the trees. Clella, broom in hand, swept the floors of
their farmhouse. It needed cleaning after they'd been gone
a year. Kenneth left earlier that morning to return to Illinois.
He had brought them back, just as he wanted, and left
them. She didn't speak to him, and he didn't seem bothered
by it.

Fifteen-year-old Linda had a terrible attitude. She
was mad at both her father and mother. Clella didn't blame
her. She knew how much Linda wanted to stay in Illinois.
Buck wasn't happy either. At twelve, he had become hard
for Clella to handle, always plunging headlong into trouble,
like the time he and Linda dared LouAnn to eat a stick of
butter. Of course, they knew what would happen. LouAnn
always accepted a dare! She ate the whole thing and got
sick as a dog. Clella held her hair out of her face when she
vomited, and comforted her until she felt well again.

But today as Clella swept, she heard all four of her
children complaining in the front yard. "You know," Clella
told them as she walked outside, "it's a beautiful summer
day. What do you say we all go swimming down at the
creek?"

"Yeah," they chimed in.

She leaned the broom against the outside of the
house and they all ran to the spring. Clella followed behind.
The kids wasted no time stripping to their undergarments.
Clella stopped at the top of the hill and watched the
excitement below. To see her children having fun soothed

her, but inside, a lump of deep sorrow settled in her throat. The sun slightly warmed her, but still she felt cold and alone. Birds sang, frogs croaked, and even the locusts hummed. The occasional splash of Buck or LouAnn interrupted the babbling stream.

Clella started down the stone steps she and the children made just a few years back. As she sat on the last one, she reflected on the sad state of her life. She wished her mother was here. How she would like to talk to her. Mother always listened and offered sound advice. Clella looked forward to seeing Essie later that evening. What would Essie say? Could she even possibly understand?

***

Essie looked at her sister just over the rim of her glasses. "Well, Clella, what do you suppose is wrong?"

"I don't know. You know how he is, always charming the ladies. I even thought he may be having an affair."

"Oh, I don't think he would, do you?" Essie asked as she helped her sister put away the canned green beans and peaches she brought her.

"He was never home," Clella explained, but how could Essie understand? Jim didn't drink and would never be caught gambling his hard-earned money away. She loved Essie more than any of her other sisters, but how could she expect her to understand. She never experienced anything like this.

"Well, did he say he would send for you when he could?"

Clella shook her head. "Sometimes, I thought maybe he just didn't feel good. He complained a lot about his chest burning. When he's around me, he complains, but when he's with Wallace and his friends, he acts like he's sixteen again. No, I think maybe there's someone else."

They changed the subject when the kids ran inside to one of the bedrooms. "Guess what your little sister and her husband are doing?" Essie asked. She had a smile on her face and a twinkle in her eye, and she chuckled.

"How are Mag and Ed?" Clella asked.

"They bought a tavern. Just off the square in Mountain Grove."

"No! Really?" Clella gasped. "Mother would roll over in her grave!"

"Isn't that the truth?" Essie agreed.

Clella and the children spent the next few weeks of summer trying to get settled and restock the house. Trips to the squares in Hartville and Mountain Grove gave Clella and the kids time to spend meeting old friends. One day in Mountain Grove, Clella saw Mag and Ed.

"We just live over on South Street," Mag said. "All our girls will be going to school this year in Mountain Grove." Mag had three girls, Patricia, Sandra, and Catherine Sue. "Maybe Pat and Linda will have some classes together," Mag added. Pat and Linda were the same age, as were Catherine Sue and LouAnn. When Clella shared how much she and the kids missed Illinois and didn't really want to be on the farm, Mag listened.

Later that evening after dinner, Clella sat on the front porch and listened to the sounds of nighttime in the summer. Locusts, frogs, and lightning bugs created a country symphony of sound and light.

Without a neighbor within yelling distance, she couldn't have been lonelier. She reflected on seeing Mag today. Mag and Ed lived in town in a cute little house with indoor plumbing. Their kids didn't have to worry about catching the bus; they could walk to school. Though she didn't share her and Kenneth's troubles with her younger sister, she now thought to herself that perhaps Mag would come nearer to understanding than anyone else. She hadn't heard from Kenneth. *Guess I'll write to him tomorrow,* she thought. Clella heard Cecil's cattle bellowing in the pasture. Kenneth had rented the pasture out last year. Cecil came by that day and paid Clella for the upcoming quarter. At least now she wouldn't be waking up early to take care of livestock.

The idea came to her as quickly as lightning. She thought about all possibilities. Yes. Why, yes. She could do this! She had Cecil's rent money and she still had a little money left from her father's estate. Suddenly, she felt empowered, almost liberated. For the first time in a long time, the ache in her heart and the lump in her throat disappeared. She would start first thing in the morning.

That night, she didn't cry herself to sleep. She rose early, gave the children chores to do in her absence, then drove into Mountain Grove. She was looking for a house to rent. By that afternoon, she had paid the first month's rent on a little house on the south side of town. It had electricity, a stove and refrigerator, and most importantly, indoor plumbing.

She was so excited. She couldn't wait to get home and tell the children. She felt like the woman in Proverbs 31, the one who rises early and buys a parcel of land and provides for her family and whose husband has no need for spoil. Suddenly, the smile left her face. Yes, she would write him today. How she wished she could see him face to face and tell him her exciting news. She missed him so much.

Dear Kenneth,

The kids and I rented a house in Mountain Grove. It's right off of Main Street and has three bedrooms. It has electricity, a stove that is like new, and a refrigerator. Linda is excited, and Buck is hoping to get an after-school job. Please come home. We miss you. I miss you.

Love,

Clella

Chapter Twenty-One

School started and still Clella hadn't heard from Kenneth. She kept herself busy sewing the kids' clothes. This year, she would buy a store-bought outfit or two. Buck grew like crazy and she couldn't keep him in long enough pants. Linda started her sophomore year. Pat, Sandra, and Catherine Sue spent time at Clella's because Mag and Ed were busy at the tavern.

The Panther football games reminded Clella of the days when Wallace and Alan played and Audrey and Alan dated. The band played as Clella and Larry climbed the stands and took a seat. Linda was cheerleading. Buck and LouAnn sat with their friends a few rows up.

"Clella, is that you?" Eva Hicks, now Eva Davis, called out from where she sat just two rows down and to the left.

"Eva, it's good to see you," Clella lied.

"I heard you were back. Someone said you moved into town."

"Yes." The crowd cheered as the home team scored.

"Is Kenny here?" Something told Clella that Eva knew the answer to that question before she asked. That was the problem with small towns. Probably everybody in Wright County knew her husband was through with her. How dare Eva call him "Kenny" like he and she were chums?

"No, he's still in Illinois working at Caterpillar."

"Oh, that's too bad. That must be really hard on you." Eva's tone contained a hint of sarcasm.

"Not at all. Enjoy the game, Eva." Clella turned her attention to Linda and her cheerleading squad. How well she cheered and she looked very cute, but Clella had to fight back the tears. She blinked repeatedly to prevent them from spilling down her cheeks. How embarrassing. Here at the game were many people she knew, but she felt lost, isolated, and alone. She prayed no one else would speak to her for she might not be able to hold herself together.

During the fourth quarter with just seconds left on the clock, she looked for Buck where she last saw him sitting. He was nowhere in sight. She walked all over the bleachers and searched the parking lot.

"Johnny, have you seen Buck?" she asked a classmate.

"No, Mrs. Lathrom. Not recently."

The game ended and Linda laughed as she walked out to the car with a group of girls. "Linda, do you know where your brother is?"

"No, huh uh."

One of the girls spoke up, "Mrs. Lathrom, I think I saw him leave with some other boys."

There was nothing for her to do but to take the rest of her family home without her son. She sat up that night and listened to the clock tick. Her mind wouldn't stop. Where was Buck? What was he doing? She could only wait. In the still of the night, she thought about her husband. Buck was his son, too. He should be here–they should be together raising their children. How was it that Kenneth escaped all this? Instead, she had to deal with it all.

At 2:30 in the morning, Buck came dragging in.

"Hi, Mommy!" he said, stumbling over the coffee table leg and grinning from ear to ear.

"Don't you 'Hi, Mommy,' me!" She would have disciplined him right there, which, in his younger years, would have included a switching with a little peach tree limb, but not tonight. She got a whiff of strong liquor and knew the best thing now would be for him to go to bed. In the morning, she'd make sure he knew the error of his ways.

Again, she cried herself to sleep. There was still no word from Kenneth. Her daughter told her in a letter, "Dad is working hard and has a doctor's appointment next week." What in the world was going on with him? Audrey had written, "We don't see him much. He spends his evenings with that same crowd."

Clella intentionally rattled pots and pans while cooking breakfast. Confident this wasn't Buck's first taste of beer or whiskey, and she fully wanted him to experience the consequences of his actions; if his head pounded fiercely, then so much the better.

He slowly entered the kitchen. With his eyes squinted, he winced whenever a loud noise occurred, but he never complained. LouAnn and Larry sat down at the table.

"Where did you go last night, Buck?" LouAnn asked. "Momma looked everywhere for you."

Clella stared straight at him and he lowered his head. "I was with John A., and Donnie, and some of the other guys."

"Don't you think you should've told me?" Clella asked. "Sometimes you act like you don't have the sense God gave a goose."

"Well, see, I knew if I asked, you'd just say no. The other guys didn't have to tell their folks and I didn't want to be different."

"Oh, I see," she said and banged the skillet on the stove for fried eggs.

"Mom, could you please not be so loud?"

"No, Son, I wouldn't want this morning to be any quieter than any other morning 'cause I know how much you don't want to be different!"

Linda finally woke up and joined them. She and Buck kept smirking, like they had their own personal joke going on that no one else knew about, especially Clella. Every so often Linda laughed. Clella knew she was losing control of her children, and they were still so young. Each day just kept getting harder.

"Well, I don't know what the two of you are up to, but you can start the day by raking the leaves in the yard."

That evening, while Clella sat in the living room with LouAnn and Larry, and Linda and Buck were away, a knock came at the door. She turned the porch light on and recognized the silhouette of Clarence, her brother-in-law and chief of police. Clarence had married her older sister, Ola. *What could he want this time of the evening?*

She opened the door. "Good evening, Clarence. Come in." She noticed Linda and Buck standing behind him. He took his hat off and came inside. "Is anything wrong?" she asked.

"As a matter of fact, there is," he said. "Clella, I found these two smashing pumpkins on Mrs. White's porch. Just made an awful mess."

"Oh, my." She looked at them both. *I could just wring their necks,* she thought. *How dare they embarrass me like this!*

"And, I'm afraid that's not the only house they got," he continued.

"Oh, Clarence, I don't know what to do." She felt she might actually start crying.

"Well, we got eye witnesses, but no one is pressing charges. I just wanted to bring them to you."

"I appreciate it."

Later, while she tried to reason with her two oldest at home, things escalated out of control.

"This is all your fault," Linda accused her mother. "If we were still in Illinois, things would be different."

"How is that my fault?"

"Because of you, Dad brought us back here," Buck said.

"I didn't want to come back. It's what your father wanted."

"No, it wasn't. I don't know what you did, but you must've made him mad," Buck yelled.

"That's right. He loves us. He wouldn't have brought us back here if it weren't for you," Linda screamed. "I hate you."

"That's enough. I don't want to hear anymore. Go to your rooms." Clella's hands shook. Her heart pounded and tears threatened to fall. She grabbed her purse and truck keys and left the house. In the truck, she started crying. It was the last straw. All she had were her kids, and they hated her.

She didn't think about God or the fact she hadn't prayed in a very long time. Nor did she remember: "He was a very present help in time of need." Instead, she clung to the hurt and anger in her heart.

She didn't plan it. She just automatically drove to the stop sign at the end of South Main and parked outside the little tavern that Mag and Ed owned. She wiped the tears from her face, put on some lipstick and got out of the car. She walked inside and immediately saw Mag behind the bar.

"Hi, Sis. Come on in." Clella sat on one of the bar stools.

"Are you okay?" Mag asked.

"I don't think so."

"What can I get you?"

Clella wasn't a drinker, but her mouth opened and she said, "I'll have a beer." She and Mag sat down at one of the booths. Over the next hour and a half, she told her sister about her troubles.

"You poor thing!" Mag listened and consoled her. "I always thought Kenneth to be a good husband and father, but I guess I didn't know a lot." They drank their beers, smoked cigarettes, and Clella left with a little lighter burden.

Chapter Twenty-Two

Watch and pray, so that you will not fall into
temptation. The spirit is willing, but the body
is weak.
...... Matthew 26:41

The next Friday evening, Clella dressed up and fixed her hair. She fastened the strand of pearls Audrey gave her for Christmas behind her neck. She clipped on matching earrings, opened a tube of lipstick, and, holding her mouth just so, colored her lips. Then she stood back and assessed herself in the mirror. She had turned forty-one only days ago, but she could pass for someone much younger. Her tiny waist sported a shiny belt just below her shapely breasts. Those who didn't know her, wouldn't have believed she had given birth to six children. *Not bad,* she thought.

She looked forward to getting out of the house and being with other adults. She left LouAnn and Larry under Linda's charge and drove to the little tavern just down from the town square.

"Clella," Mag yelled as she walked inside. The jukebox played a lively tune.

"Hi, Mag." Mag served Clella a glass of beer without even asking. Clella loved dancing, and when John Massey asked her to dance, she accepted without thinking twice. As they danced, she noticed a young man at the bar with wavy light brown hair. Whatever he said must have been funny because a couple of ladies and Ed burst into laughter. She noticed, though, that the man kept glancing in her direction.

Later, Clella sat at a booth with Mag and Ed. Laughter rumbled from the folks sitting at one of the tables in the dimly-lit tavern.

"I'm glad you're getting out some," Mag told her.

"Yeah? Well, it feels good." She looked up and couldn't resist checking out the young man at the bar again. He was looking right at her. Quickly she turned away, but from the corner of her eye, she thought she saw him heading in their direction.

"Ed, aren't you going to introduce me?" he asked.

"Why, sure, Francis, this is my sister-in-law..." Ed started, but Clella interrupted him before he could say her name.

"Catherine," she said and held out her hand. "My name is Catherine." And it was. It was her middle name. For some inexplicable reason, tonight she had a very strong desire to be someone different. Clella was married and did housework. Clella chased children and cooked and washed dishes. Clella had all this baggage and had been deserted by her husband. Tonight, she would be Catherine. Besides, she never liked her name anyway. What had her mother and father been thinking? The boys in their family had such sensible names, William and Charles, but she didn't know what possessed her parents in naming their girls!

"So, Mag, you didn't tell me you had such a pretty sister."

"I have several pretty sisters, Francis. Clel...er ...Catherine is just one of them."

"You want to join us?" Ed invited.

As Francis scooted in right next to her, Clella's heart raced.

"So, you live around here?" He stared right into her eyes. His were blue, deep pools of blue.

"Actually, just down the road a ways. You?"

"Just a couple of blocks from here." He looked at her empty glass. "Can I buy you a beer?"

Mag and Ed exchanged looks.

"Maybe I could have one more." She smiled at him. "Thanks."

"Just *one* more? The night's still young." And it was young, but not for a mother of six with four children waiting at home. For a brief moment, she thought about Kenneth. What was he doing tonight? More than likely, he was at a similar place, drinking and flirting with the ladies–or maybe with one in particular. He didn't have to worry about getting home to the kids. Music from the jukebox started again.

"Well, Catherine, do you want to dance?" "Why not?" she answered with a smile. They danced to the "Tennessee Waltz", a recording by Patti Page. They glided together beautifully. It felt so good to be on the dance floor. His arm fit around her back just perfectly.

"You're pretty good at this," he told her with a smile. She felt his eyes caress her body, and she warmed at his attention. For one night, she wasn't forty-one. She was sixteen again and having fun. She refused to let herself think about responsibilities, or age, or time, or a husband. It was as if this enticing carrot dangled in front of her, and just like a horse, she couldn't resist.

"I can't believe I haven't seen you in here before. I stop in about every day," he commented.

"I don't usually come in here. In fact, this is just the second time."

"You're kidding!"

"I'm really not much of a drinker," she told him, talking without missing a step as they danced.

"Maybe not, but you're one heck of dancer," he said as he spun her and then pulled her a little closer.

She laughed. "You're in here every day, huh? Does that make you a heavy drinker?" she asked. Their eyes focused on each other. Adrenaline rushed and excitement coursed through her veins.

"Me? Not really. Just like to get out, that's all."

The words of the song suddenly caught Clella's attention. *Yes, I lost my little darlin' the night they were playing the beautiful Tennessee Waltz.*

When the music stopped, he held her hand. They laughed and he returned with her to the booth. Mag and Ed served their patrons from behind the bar.

"I really should be getting home," Clella sighed after an awkward moment.

"You're kidding. You can't go home yet. It's not even ten o'clock."

She didn't want to leave, but the magical mist slowly evaporated as she remembered her family. Part of that reality started as she looked closely at Francis. He was fun and charming, had the bluest eyes and sexy wavy hair, but how old was he? She wasn't a good judge of age, but he must be younger than she was.

Clella picked up her sweater, and with a smile she turned to him, "It was fun, Francis. Thanks for the beer."

"Will I see you here tomorrow?"

"I doubt it."

He stood up as she practically fled from the bar. "Can I drive you home?" she heard him ask as she left.

Once inside her home, Linda and Buck asked her all kinds of questions.

"Where did you go, Mom?" Buck asked first.

"Did you have a good time?" Linda wanted to know.

"I visited Aunt Mag and Uncle Ed," she answered as she hung up her sweater. "Yes, Honey. I had a very good time."

"Good." Linda seemed satisfied. Clella couldn't help but smile as she thought about the evening. She hummed and swayed back and forth as she got dressed into her nightgown. That night, she didn't cry herself to sleep.

The next morning, Buck left early to work his newspaper route. Linda spent the day with a friend, and LouAnn went to play with Catherine Sue. As Larry watched cartoons, Clella looked out the kitchen window. The red, orange, and yellow leaves on the trees fell softly to the ground. Confusion clouded her thoughts. She remembered the years and the love of her life. She needed her husband more now than ever before. Then clearly, she understood her own vulnerability.

She opened a drawer and pulled out a tablet and pen. Then she sat down at the kitchen table and started writing.

Dear Kenneth,

I need to see you. I miss you so much. We can work this out. Please come home to your family. Please come home to me.

I love you, Clella

A week went by and no answer. Essie and Jim came into town that Saturday and stopped by to visit. At the kitchen table, over a cup of coffee, Clella told her sister, "I'm losing control of the kids, Essie. Some days are so hard."

"Have you heard from Kenny?"

Clella shook her head. "I don't think I'm going to. And if truth be told, I'm not sure I want to anymore."

Essie stared at her and opened her mouth to speak, but no words were uttered. She merely nodded and kissed her on the cheek.

After an awkward silence, Essie finally whispered, "I wish I knew what to say. I'm not sure what Kenneth Lathrom's thinking, Sis." Essie finally said softly. Clella could tell Essie was beginning to understand the seriousness of her situation.

***

That evening as her tenacity dissolved and loneliness set in, Clella decided to venture down to the tavern again. Perhaps her motivation wasn't even clear to herself. She thought she would just go say hi to her sister, but in truth, she wondered if he would be there.

When she entered, a group of musicians were playing live music. Set up in the back corner of the room, the fiddle, guitar, and drums blended in exciting sound. Clella recognized Lila Thompson, the singer. Then she saw him, playing the guitar, intent on fingering the chords and lost in the rhythm. He strummed the strings with his right hand. She noticed his arm unnaturally curved at the elbow almost backward.

She sat down and Mag brought her a beer. Without taking her eyes off Francis, she told her sister, "This place is hopping tonight."

"Yeah, what do you think?" Mag asked.

"It sounds great." Just then, Francis looked up and noticed her. She couldn't deny her attraction to him. But, if he knew she had six children and was separated from her husband, not to mention, considerably older– no, perish the thought. He couldn't be interested in her. She shouldn't even be thinking about it.

"So, what's the story with Francis?" Clella asked her sister. "Does he really come in here every night?"

"Just about. His folks are Everette and Anna Burch."

"I don't guess I know them."

"They live on Main Street. I think they work at the shoe factory."

Without taking her eyes off him, Clella nodded and muttered, "Hmm."

In a few minutes, the band took a break. Francis got a glass of beer and came and sat down across from her. She raised her eyebrows and smiled. "I didn't know you could play like that."

"I've just got that old instrument right now, but if I had a Gibson, I could really play," he told her. "Let me buy you another beer," he offered.

"No, I couldn't..." she trailed off without finishing.

"Couldn't what?" he asked. "You expecting somebody else?"

She shook her head. Nothing could be farther from the truth. "You know, Francis, you don't know anything about me."

"That's not true. I've been doing my homework. You'd be surprised what I know." He turned his head sideways and grinned.

She smiled slyly. "Oh, yeah? What did you learn?" As soon as she asked it, she wished she hadn't, for the answer would surely mean complete forthrightness. And she really liked the attention he lavished on her.

"Your name is Catherine, a.k.a. Clella Lathrom." She started to protest, but he went on. "You live over on Elm Street. You have four children and you can really dance."

She smiled and blushed. He mentioned the children and obviously had been inquiring about her. She decided to tease, "See, you don't know everything about me."

"Oh, yeah, what did I miss?" he asked.

"I don't have four children. I have six." Instantly, she regretted saying it. This would surely end whatever this was.

"You're kidding!" He stood up and walked over to the bar. He returned carrying two beers. Setting one in front of her, he sat down again.

"So where's your husband?" His blue eyes stared into hers.

"We've separated," she looked down. "He lives in Illinois. The children and I have made our home here."

"Where are the other two—what boy, girl, boys, girls?" He started to take a drink of his beer.

"One of each, and they're grown," she answered.

He almost choked and his eyes widened. He quickly lowered his glass. "How old *are* you?"

She shifted nervously. "How old do you think I am?"

Francis looked at her thoughtfully. He sort of laughed and answered, "You don't look a day over twenty-nine. However, I've never struggled with arithmetic, and unless you started at ten, that's probably not your age."

"Well, okay, how old are *you*?" she asked.

"No. No. I asked first." Then he paused.

"How old do you think I am?"

"Hum," she thought, "Thirty-two or thirty-three."

He slammed his glass down on the table. "Close enough," he said. The other players were setting up again. He stood up and put some money on the table. "You going to stick around?"

"Just for a little while."

"Are you free tomorrow afternoon?" he asked.

"Maybe. Why?"

"I wanted to show you a place in the country." He reached in his pocket and pulled out a guitar pick.

"I don't know, Francis," she hesitated. "It might not be such a good idea. There are obviously differences in our ages."

"Yeah, I thought we established that. I'm thirty-three and you're twenty-nine. Perfect." He laughed. "I'll pick you up here at noon."

Chapter Twenty-Three

But I say unto you, that whosoever shall put
away his wife, saving for the cause of
fornication, causeth her to commit adultery:
......Matthew 5:32 KJV

The next day, Clella arrived on time and parked down the street a ways from the tavern. Francis was waiting. He jumped out and opened the door for her, smiling as he took notice of her floral print dress with belted waist and flowing skirt. Once behind the steering wheel, he stole a glance at her as he put the car in gear and sped away toward the south side of town.

The sun brightened the pleasantly warm autumn day. Apples were in full harvest throughout the countryside, and a hint of cinnamon filled the air. He drove out of town and onto the dirt road heading southeast.

"Where are we going?" she asked.

"You'll see."

She smiled. He stretched his arm behind her and let it rest on the back of the seat. She looked at him. "Where exactly are you taking me? Are your intentions honorable, Mr. Burch?" she asked and laughed.

"Never, Kid. With the way you look today, my intentions are anything but honorable!"

The car rolled through a creek that crossed the road and meandered through a beautiful valley. She had never been in this part of the country before. After a short distance, he pulled the car over and into a field. He grabbed a basket out of the back seat, then went around and opened her door.

She took the hand he offered, and he led her down a pathway to a stream. They crossed it, stepping onto stones big enough to allow them to cross over the water without getting wet. Clella's foot slipped once, and he caught her as she grabbed his arm.

"You all right?" he asked.

She nodded and clung to him. He stopped under a big oak tree shrouded in hues of orange, red, and yellow. He spread a quilt on the ground, and they both sat down.

"What do you think?" he quizzed her.

She looked all around her. "It's beautiful." The water rushed over the rocks. The grass was still green and waved slightly as a gentle breeze raked through it. The autumn leaves rustled in the trees, and birds serenaded them with a myriad of melodies.

"I grew up here," he told her.

"You did? It looks like rich farmland."

He shook his head, "It's not." And then he added with emphasis, "Trust me. Beneath two inches of soil there's nothing but rock. It's very hard land to work." He opened the basket and pulled out fried chicken and potato salad. He brought some watermelon, too."

"Wow! That looks really good."

"Dig in," he said, handing her a plate. They sat for a moment enjoying the food. Then, he broke the silence. "I went to school just over that hill," he pointed, "but only until the sixth grade."

"Where did you go to school after that?"

"I didn't."

"You only went to the sixth grade?" She couldn't believe it. He didn't seem uneducated.

"Yep. I was lucky they let me go that long. I got sent home one day for kicking the socks off the teacher."

She laughed, making him laugh, too. "You did what?"

"Well, I didn't like her." They both ate a moment, stealing a quick look at the other one here and there. Finally, Francis spoke again. "No, talking about this land, when I was fifteen, I couldn't take it anymore. My old man and I got into it and I left."

"You sound like somewhat of a rebel," she stated. "So what did you do when you left?"

"I hitchhiked to Oregon. I stopped at this one orchard, looking for work. They told me they didn't have anything. But, they had loaded this big truck with apples and it was in the way. They needed it moved. I don't know where the driver went, but the boss was yelling, 'Does anybody know how to drive this truck?' Well, I needed work, so I figured this was my chance. I hollered, 'Yes, Sir, I do.'" He laughed. "I hopped in and the thing had about eight gears."

"Did you know how to drive it?"

"Of course not!" He laughed again. "I had never driven before, but somehow I figured it out and got a job to boot."

"Really?" she watched him, amazed at his story. The sun caught his hair and glistened on flecks of gold. "So you drove trucks for the orchard?" she asked.

"Oh, yeah, and not just them. After that, I got a job for Smith Trucking. They haul cars across country."

"Wow. I envy you. I've never been anywhere but Missouri and Illinois. I've always wanted to go places like out west or to New Mexico. Have you been to New Mexico?"

"Yep. I've been everywhere west of the Mississippi." He looked at her as her eyes widened. The wind gently blew her hair, and she smiled at him.

"But, you're not driving now, are you?" she asked.

"No, but that's a long story." He paused a moment before going on.

She reached out and touched his arm. "Tell me," she coaxed.

"I was married. I really loved her. I left to go on a trip and returned a little sooner than planned. I found her in the arms of another man. I kind of lost the appetite for driving trucks after that."

"What happened?"

"We got a divorce. I just couldn't get past it." They stared into each other's eyes.

She broke the silence. "So, tell me what happened to your arm."

"When I was a kid, a horse threw me and then stomped on my elbow. Crushed it. The doctor tried to set it, but it turned out backward."

"Wow. How old were you?"

"About nine."

Clella looked down at her watch.

He then quickly urged, "Tell me about your kids." He stretched out on his side.

She sighed and picked up a pebble next to the quilt. "Well, Linda is in high school, boy-crazy, and not very happy with her mother at the moment. Buck, I'm afraid, is developing a taste for beer."

"Well, what's wrong with that?" Francis laughed and ducked to miss the pebble she threw at him.

"He's only thirteen!"

Still laughing, Francis added, "Sounds like the right age to me."

"No, I'm being serious. It's a real problem."

"Okay." He was still smiling, but he wasn't joking anymore. "What about the other two?"

"LouAnn is nine and doing really well in school. Larry, my youngest, has asthma and he struggles a lot."

"So, what's the story with you and your husband?"

She shook her head and looked away into the distance. "I guess he just got tired of me. He brought me and the kids here and left us. I haven't heard from him."

"You're kidding!" He shook his head. "Crazy!"

She avoided looking at him and started putting things away.

The sun disappeared below the horizon as they returned to town. Francis once again put his arm on the back of the seat. She turned to face him, and for a moment, they stared into each other's eyes. He stroked her hair and then gently caressed the side of her neck.

Her heart skipped a beat. Thrills shivered down her spine. She knew she shouldn't be with him, but whenever they were together, it felt heavenly.

After Francis parked the truck, he went around and opened her door. Her hand trembled as she fumbled for her keys. She sensed him watching her. Finally, she lifted her head, letting her eyes meet his. "I had a nice time, Francis. It was a very nice day."

He moved closer. Excitement swept over her. Her heart raced. Slowly, he reached out and lifted her chin. Her breath caught in her throat. A brief stab of guilt caved to a stronger longing to be loved. Try as she may, she couldn't resist.

Closing the final distance between them, he gently kissed her, and she experienced a joy lost to her for the past several years. She never wanted it to end, for in that kiss, nothing else existed except him and her. When he finally pulled away, she left with a smile on her face. She knew he was watching her as she walked to her truck.

"Hey, Kid?" he called, and she turned around. "Am I going to see you tomorrow?"

"We'll see," she answered.

"Here?"

"Maybe," she said teasingly before driving away.

She pulled in the driveway and turned off the ignition. She sat there and stared at the house. Inside were teenagers and children, conflict, work, chaos, more work, sorrow, and work. She didn't want to go in. She thought about the day. What was she doing? Oh, my goodness, what was she doing? She needed to put a stop to it right now before it went any further. For her to get involved with

Francis would only mean more trouble, and she had enough troubles already.

The next couple of weeks passed slowly. Every day, she waited anxiously for the postman, hoping for a letter from Illinois; none came, except from Audrey. Even she didn't write as often as usual. Clella could tell her two grandsons kept her oldest daughter very busy. Audrey did write that Alan worked evenings and she worked days so they could take care of the boys without a babysitter. Clella wondered if that was wise for a couple so young to hardly ever see each other.

Chapter Twenty-Four

A wintery cloud cover blew in during the afternoon before Clella went to pick the kids up from school on that chilly November day. She drove to the elementary school first, and LouAnn and Larry climbed in the car. Larry looked pale and peaked.

"How was school today?" she asked them.

"I won the math competition, Mom," LouAnn told her mother. Her eyes beamed and she smiled from ear to ear.

"That's great, Honey!" Clella exclaimed. Larry coughed and Clella recognized that sound.

"We'd better get home and get you some medicine," she told him.

As she drove in front of the high school, she didn't see Linda at her usual spot. She waited for a while, but Larry kept coughing. She knew she needed to get him home. He struggled harder with each breath. Clella let the truck roll past the school when she noticed a group of kids a little distance from the side of the building. There was Linda, taking a puff from the cigarette in her hand. Clella parked and jumped out. She walked to the front of the pickup.

"Linda!" she yelled. "Come on, let's go." Linda turned her back to the road as if that would conceal her actions. She threw the cigarette down and stepped on it, twisting her foot slightly. Grabbing her books, she turned and ran for the truck.

"Hi, Mother. Sorry, I didn't know you were waiting." Linda climbed in the vehicle, acting as if she'd not been caught in the act.

"What do you think you were doing?" Clella asked. "I saw you smoking."

"Oh, Mother, it's nothing. We all do it."

"No, Linda. Nice girls don't smoke."

"You do it." Her words rang true. Should Clella expect her daughter to act better than the example she provided?

"Linda, I don't want to see you smoking again. Do you understand?" Clella argued with her daughter until they got home.

Once inside their home, Larry, who struggled for air, required her complete attention.

Almost a week passed before Larry got better. Clella watched over him day and night. She had done this so many times during the six years of young life. Between fighting with Linda and Buck staying out until all hours of the night, Clella thought she might actually lose her mind. She felt so utterly alone in her struggles with her children.

One day in the middle of November, the whistle at Brown Shoe Factory sounded just like clockwork at noon, signaling a lunch break for the workers. Usually, not too long after the whistle blew, the mailman delivered Clella's mail. As she checked the box just outside the door, she really didn't expect much, but found a letter from Audrey. Clella opened it and read anxiously. Just like always when she received something from her daughter, she expected some news about Kenneth.

Audrey wrote about Al and Van, work, and then toward the end of the letter came the news. Caterpillar was requiring mandatory overtime of all employees over the holiday weekend. They would have Thursday off, but would have to work on Friday and Saturday. They wouldn't be able to come for Thanksgiving. Clella let the letter fall from her hand. She walked over to the window by the sink and stared outside at the gray day. The remnants of last week's first snowfall were melting away. Tears streamed down her cheeks.

That evening, she left her children to go to the
tavern. As she walked in, she quickly surveyed the room.
Mag smiled, obviously glad to see her.

"I tell ya, Clella. I'm just working all the time," her
sister told her as they both sat and drank a couple of beers.

"I'm sorry, Mag. I know it must be hard." Clella kept
looking at the door each time it opened. "Where's Francis?
Doesn't he usually come in here in the evenings?"

"He hasn't been here in a while." She noticed Mag
look at her with scrutiny. "He kept asking about you, too.
Then he just stopped coming in."

"Hum, I wonder what happened?" Clella asked. She
looked away and took another drink of her beer. Her heart
sank. She had stayed away, taking care of her family, trying
to be strong. Now, she would probably never see him again.
It was foolishness in the first place, she thought.

Just then, the door opened and Francis walked
inside and stepped up to the bar.

"Well, speaking of the devil," Mag said as she got up
to ask him what he'd like, leaving Clella alone, but not
unnoticed.

"I'll have a beer, Mag." Francis took his glass and
walked over to Clella.

"May I sit down?" he asked too formally. He wasn't
smiling. As he sat down, he spoke again, "May I ask a
question?"

"Of course."

"What did I do wrong?"

His frankness took her by surprise. "Francis, you
didn't do anything wrong. As a matter of fact, you did
everything pretty darn near right."

"Then why did you say you would meet me and
then not show up? For weeks?"

"I just don't think it's wise for us to continue to see
each other."

"Then why are you here?"

"My sister owns this place, remember?"

"I don't think that's it. I think you thought I would be here."

"Really? Well, I have it on good authority that you haven't been here. I think you just stopped in today because you saw I was here. What do you think about that?" She squinted her eyes, but smiled slyly.

"You have it on good authority, huh? I think that just proves my point." He rose suddenly and took his beer with him. She watched him walk away. Surely, she had discouraged him from pursuing her. It stirred feelings of regret. She watched as he went to the jukebox and dropped some coins in the slot. Then he slowly walked back over to her table, set his beer down, reached out his hand and asked, "You want to dance?"

She didn't say a word, but stood without taking her eyes off him. She walked into his arms and he swept her away. She got lost somewhere between the rhythm of the song, the warmth of his arms, and the security of his cheek next to hers. The very elements of companionship she so desperately needed flowed from his hands into hers, mending the ache in her heart.

Later, she left the bar in the arms of this younger man. Once inside the confines of his car, they embraced. He kissed her, and she kissed him back. She ran her fingers through his wavy hair. His hands found the curves of her body. She gasped and pulled away, searching his face. No, she shouldn't be doing this, but God help her, she couldn't resist. It felt so good to be held. Her lips once again sought his as she completely surrendered to her overwhelming desire.

***

The next time she saw him, she was shopping at the square in Mountain Grove, and he just happened to be there. They hadn't planned it. He walked toward her with a smile.

"What are you doing later tonight?" he asked, his blue eyes fixed on her.

"What did you have in mind?" She smiled slyly.

"Meet me at Mag's?" he suggested.

"About eight?" She asked and took a quick look around. She noticed a couple of people taking interest in them. As he nodded, she half turned and whispered, "I'll see you then."

She bought groceries at Richards Brothers and then headed to the soda fountain in the drugstore. The kids had walked to town earlier to see *Roman Holiday,* starring Gregory Peck and Audrey Hepburn, at the movie theater on the square. She figured they'd probably all be drinking a cherry coke by now at the soda fountain in Sam's Drugstore.

Sam said the kids were there, but they had left. A group of people came running inside the store. "Is Clella Lathrom in here?" one of the ladies yelled.

"I'm right here," she answered. Alarmingly, they all tried to talk at the same time. Clella caught only part of what they said. "Little boy walking across street...hit by a car...took him to Barber Funeral Home."

"Oh, my God!" Clella gasped and ran out. Even though she had parked nearby, she ran straight for the funeral home, one block off the square. All kinds of thoughts rushed through her mind. *Oh, please, God. No. Don't let him be dead.* But, why else would he be at the funeral home? She must be dreaming–a nightmare. Her legs kept moving, but she felt like she wasn't getting anywhere. Out of breath and heart pounding, she ran into the front door of the funeral parlor.

She saw Linda and LouAnn, crying, but no sign of Larry. LouAnn ran and hugged her mother. "Oh, Mommy, it was awful," LouAnn said through tears.

Clella turned to Linda as she frantically looked around. "Where is he?"

Instead of answering, Linda despondently told her mother, "Larry wanted ice cream. He just walked out in front of this car."

"Oh, my God, no." She shook Linda's shoulders. "Where is he?"

Mr. Barber entered the hall and met Clella. "Come with me, Mom, he's in here." Clella couldn't make her feet move. He put his arm around her and walked along beside her. She went weak in the knees. She couldn't bear to see the lifeless body of her youngest boy who struggled from birth just to be able to breathe.

As they entered the left parlor room, Clella gasped as Larry lay in one of the coffins. Her heart couldn't sink any lower. She could now identify with the ache of parents who lose their children. What would she do now?

"I think he's okay, Clella," Mr. Barber said. "I checked him and I don't think he even broke a bone. Course, you might want to have Doc look at him, though."

Larry opened his eyes at the sound of their entrance, and Clella let out the breath she held. At that moment, her legs went out from under her and she landed on the soft cushion of a pew on the right. Larry sat up. "Mommy, my pennies are somewhere in the street. I just wanted an ice cream cone." She was crying but she managed to get up, run to him, and lift him out of the coffin.

"Yes, but are you all right? Are you hurt anywhere?"

"I scraped my knee, but Mr. Barber put a Bandaid on it."

She hugged him tight. "Thank you, Mr. Barber," she said and hugged the older gentleman, too. Then, she led her son out of the funeral home. Together, she, Linda, LouAnn, and Larry walked slowly back to the car.

Chapter Twenty-Five

*I know that nothing good lives in me, that is,
in my sinful nature.
For I have the desire to do what is good, but I
cannot carry it out.
......Romans 7:18*

That afternoon, she thought about the meeting she and Francis planned. She would go and break it off. It was the only thing for her do. It was all wrong. She knew that. She must end this madness, even though it would be one of the most difficult things she had ever done.

Francis sat at the bar, drinking a beer. Three other apparently unattached pretty ladies also sat at the bar. Clella took a seat at a booth. She motioned to Mag that she didn't want anything to drink. He came over and sat across from her.

"Aren't you going to have something to drink?" he asked.

"No, Francis. I have to get back home."

"What's your hurry?" he signaled for Mag to bring over a drink.

"My son was hit by a car today."

"You're kidding? Is he all right?" He reached out and placed his hand on top of hers. She looked at it. How she yearned to tell Kenneth about Larry and how much it scared her, but here, another man offered her comfort instead.

"Luckily, he's fine. But the point is, I've been thinking. And this here, you and me, it's not going to work." She pointed to him and to herself and then back again.

"Don't say that. It is working."

"Francis, I have four children at home and I haven't kidded myself into thinking that this relationship can go any further than where it is now."

"I don't know why not. I don't have anything against kids. Unless, you just don't like me," he seemed sincerely hurt.

"Well, then there's the little thing of our ages," she said tentatively. Could he possibly think it would work?

"How old are you? Thirty-seven?" he asked. She swallowed hard before answering.

"Forty-one." He almost choked on his drink.

"How old are you?" she asked.

"I'm not sure I want to answer that," he replied. "Look, I like you. I like being with you. I don't want us to end. You seem like you need someone in your life right now and I'm just glad to be the one."

"How old are you?" she persisted.

He looked at her a long time before answering. "I'll be twenty-eight in April."

"Oh, no," she uttered. "I'm almost old enough to be your mother." She grabbed her purse and slid out of the booth.

"Catherine? Wait," he called after her. She didn't stop. She walked right out the door and down the street. She could hear his footsteps as he ran behind her. "Stop," he reached out and grabbed her arm, swinging her around to face him. "Don't leave like this. Let's just talk a minute."

"Francis, you're nice looking, talented, funny, and young. You could have any one of those pretty girls in there right now."

"But, it's not them I want." He reached for her hand. "It's you. You're the one I want, Catherine."

She looked into his bright blue eyes and saw the agony in them. She, too, felt the same despair. What had she gotten herself into? She never once dreamed there might be almost fourteen years between them. She pulled away. "I must go."

He would've believed she didn't care for him, but the tears proved otherwise. Just the same, he let her go. They both needed to sort things out.

***

Despite December being one of the happiest times of the year, Clella had never been more depressed. It had been almost two weeks since she had seen Francis, and yet thoughts of him consumed her. She no longer watched her mailbox for letters from Illinois. All she could think about was how life had tempted her with something she couldn't have. Not only did her husband find her undesirable, but now she had to accept she was too old to love this wavy haired, adventurous musician.

She scrubbed floors, cleaned windows, washed bedding, darned socks, but all the work in the world didn't prevent her yearning for more of that little taste of ecstasy she found with Francis.

It was Wednesday, and the kids were at school. The whistle blew at the shoe factory, demanding everyone return to work after lunch. Even the whistle reminded her of Francis because his mother and father worked there. She took a deep breath and decided to turn on the radio. She heard a knock at the door. When she opened it, there he stood with a grin on his face. Then they heard the strains of "The Sunny Side of the Street" on the radio.

"Grab your hat and get your coat," he told her, almost in unison with the song. "Leave your troubles on the doorstep. We're going out," he coaxed. "To the sunny side of the street," the song played.

She laughed. Truth was that when she opened the door, her spirits lifted about ten feet. He didn't have to convince her further.

***

That Saturday morning, Clella slept longer than usual. She could hear the television and knew LouAnn and Larry were watching Saturday morning cartoons. She threw back the covers and felt the cold air before pulling on her robe and stepping into her slippers.

"No, I don't want to watch Popeye," LouAnn screamed. She and Larry wrestled in front of the television. Clella sighed and ran her hand through her unruly hair.

"You just want to watch Mickey Mouse. I never get to watch what I want," Larry argued and then pulled her hair as she moved to change the channel. She screamed again.

"That's enough! Just turn it off if you can't share," Clella said, and then looked around the house. "Where's Linda and Buck?"

"Linda went shopping," LouAnn told her mother. "I don't know where Buck went."

"Mom, it's not fair. Larry always gets to watch what he wants and I never do." The arguing began again. Clella walked over and turned the television off.

"Now, make your beds and get dressed. Then, you can go outside and play."

Clella put on a pot of coffee as an awful headache formed. She also scrambled some eggs and made toast. As she spread preserves on a slice, she heard a knock at the front door.

Larry opened the door. "Aunt Essie," he said.

Clella hugged Essie and poured her sister a cup of coffee. They each sat down at the small table in the kitchen and had a piece of toast with strawberry preserves.

"How have you been, Clella?" Essie asked.

"Fine. Fine. The kids are sometimes a handful, but they like living in town." There was so much she wanted to tell her sister, but she knew Essie would never understand. Clella didn't think Essie would judge, but she definitely wouldn't understand.

"I talked to Mag yesterday," Essie said.

Oh, great. Here it comes, she thought. "Oh, yeah, what did she have to say?"

"I told her I hadn't seen you much and she said she sees you quite often."

"I go in there from time to time. It's nice to talk to adults once in a while."

They each took a drink of coffee to fill the awkward moment.

Essie spoke again. "Mag said something about you and a guitar player. She said the two of you had developed quite a friendship." It seemed Essie chose her words cautiously, but Clella knew what she meant.

"She's talking about Francis. He's a nice young man."

"Clella, you can't seriously be thinking about..." Clella interrupted her.

"Now, Essie, just stop right there. This is none of your business," Clella said. "I'm doing the best I can here."

"I don't mean anything, Clella. I just want you to think about what you're doing." Essie set her coffee cup down as the tension between them grew. "If Kenny knew..."

Clella held up her hand. "Stop! You mean if Kenny cared! Which, obviously he doesn't because I haven't heard a word from him."

"Clella, all couples go through a time like this," Essie reasoned.

"A time like what? I've written him, Essie, and asked him to come home. I've told him how much I need him and still nothing."

Essie nodded, and they sat in silence. Then Essie stood and patted Clella on the shoulder. "I just don't want you to do something you'll regret later." Essie kissed Clella on the forehead and told LouAnn and Larry goodbye before letting herself out the front door.

Chapter Twenty-Six

*You may be sure that your sin will find you
out.*
......Numbers 32:23

That evening, Clella slipped into her black dress with
the low neckline. She brushed her hair before pinning her
black hat in place. She pulled the netting down in front and
colored her lips. Then she put on a sleek pair of gloves,
smoothing them up over her elbows.

She knelt over Larry's bed, where he lay sleeping
and kissed his cheek. She pulled the covers up over
LouAnn's shoulders and kissed her forehead.

"Where are you going, Mommy?" LouAnn asked.

"I've been invited to a party. I shouldn't be long and
I'll be here when you wake up in the morning." Clella smiled
and closed the bedroom door. When she turned, she came
face to face with Linda.

"I probably won't be home until after midnight,"
she told her. "I have to drive to Lebanon. Don't have any
kids over and get to bed at a decent hour." After all, Linda
was sixteen and quite capable of babysitting. Clella had lied,
telling her about a birthday party of a longtime friend.

"We'll be fine, Mom," Linda assured her.

"I don't know when Buck will be home from
Ronnie's, but it shouldn't be too long."

Clella started the truck and headed to their
rendezvous point. It had become too conspicuous for them
to meet outside Mag and Ed's tavern. Everybody talked in
small towns. She drove about five miles outside of town
before pulling over. He wasn't there. She turned the car off
and waited in the silence and cold. What she was doing
might not be right, but it was too late now. She was crazy

about this young man who played the guitar, laughed with her, and made her feel young again. It had become so much more than just her need to get out, to escape the troubles of her life, or even her desire to show Kenneth she could be attractive, too. Francis stirred feelings in her she never knew she had.

She saw the headlights and noticed the car slowing down. This would be him. He pulled over and she got out. He met her in the light of his headlights.

"Hi, Kid," he said. Strange that he should call *her* kid, just like Humphrey Bogart in Casablanca. He called her that even though she was older than he was. She liked it. It made her feel just a little bit like Ingrid Bergman.

"Hi, yourself," she smiled as she walked into his arms. They kissed on that dark, deserted stretch of back road between Mountain Grove and Cabool. When the kiss ended, her longing matched that in his eyes, but they had someplace to be.

"You ready?" Francis finally asked.

"I'm ready," she answered. They got into his car. They weren't going to some party in Lebanon, like she had told her children. Gossip traveled fast and she knew she needed to be more careful. Instead, they were going to a bar in Cabool where Francis was playing guitar with a group of local musicians. She could listen to him play all night.

"You know, this guy who will be there tonight, he and I played in an amateur contest in St. Louis once," Francis told her as they drove in the dark.

"Oh, yeah? How did you do?"

He put his arm around her and pulled her closer to him. "We won. And would have collected five hundred dollars but Johnny had played once at a club on the south side of St. Louis and got paid for it."

"So?"

"Well, if you've gotten paid to play, then you're considered a professional not an amateur. And," he shook his head, "it was a contest for amateurs."

"That's awful."

"You're telling me! I could've used my part of that money."

When they arrived, Francis introduced Clella as Catherine to the band. She sat at a table up close and sipped her beer. She watched Francis as he talked with the guys and cracked a few jokes. She listened to them tuning their instruments, which seemed to take a long time. Then just before they started, he looked at her and winked. She laughed and swayed with the rhythm as the room came alive with music—popular tunes, songs made famous by recording artists like Ernest Tubb, Hank Williams, and Bob Wills.

She enjoyed watching him play. As much fun as they had together, she still knew it wouldn't last. He wasn't happy here in the Ozarks. He always told her that just as soon as he could, he was leaving this town. But for now, she didn't care. She would hang onto what happiness she could find for as long as possible.

Later, as they drove home, he pulled over and like two high school kids, they made out in the car.

***

Another cold night in February and once again, Buck's mother got ready to leave home. He and Linda had become suspicious.

Sitting on the sofa next to him, Linda whispered, "Where do you think she's going?"

"I don't know, but I'm going to find out." Buck had concocted a plan.

"What are you going to do?"

He raised his finger to his lips. "Shh." he warned as his mom walked into the room. "You'll see."

Clella reached for her coat and scarf. "I'll be back before long."

"Have a good time, Mom," Buck told her and grabbed his coat, too. "I'm going over to Ronnie's for an hour or so," he said so she wouldn't suspect what he was about to do.

While Buck pulled his gloves over his fingers, he heard his mother telling Linda, "I made some cookies. They're in the kitchen if you guys get hungry for a snack." He slipped out into the cold and climbed into the back of the pickup, lying flat, hoping not to be noticed.

Buck heard the front door close and his mother's footsteps coming closer. The truck door opened and shut. The engine started and they began moving. His heart pounded, but she apparently hadn't noticed him. The cold wind whipped into the bed of the truck. Soon, the streetlights ended. Pitch black swallowed him as even the stars dared not shine.

As the truck pulled over, light from somewhere illuminated the trees on the side of the road. The engine turned off and his mother got out of the vehicle. He lifted his head just enough to look through the back window and spy on her.

Another car faced them with its lights on. A man got out and crossed in front to open the passenger door.

"Come on, we're going to be late," he said. Buck stifled a gasp. The stranger embraced and kissed his mother—a kiss that shouldn't have happened and lasted way too long!

Buck's eyes widened and his heart sank as he took in the sight.

"Sorry, I'm late..." he heard Mom say to this man, this unknown man, who closed the door and drove her away.

Buck sat for a moment, stunned. Then he jumped over the side of the pickup. He curled his hands into fists, kicked the tires and the dirt, and pounded his fist into the side door.

He had wanted to find out what she was up to. Now, he wished he didn't know. He opened the door and peered at the ignition. He would chase after them if he could, but she had taken the keys. He didn't want to wait for her to return, but which way was home? Finally, he began walking in the opposite direction. In the bitter cold night, Buck only felt the heat of betrayal.

***

When Clella returned home later, Linda and Buck met her. She thought it strange they should still be awake, but what happened next caught her completely off guard.

"Mommy, how could you?" Buck's voice cracked.

His face was drawn and his eyes were moist. Clella's heart skipped a beat. "What?"

"He was there," Linda said through clenched teeth. "He saw everything."

"Who was that man?" Buck asked. Realization fell hard like a two-ton brick, and her pulse raced. Looking at her son and daughter, she saw the hurt in their eyes.

"You both don't understand," she started.

"I understand," Linda's teeth were still clenched. "I'm not babysitting for you ever again. All the while, you're having some sordid fling with..." Linda's voice changed to almost a plea. "How could you do this to Daddy?"

Clella raised her voice. "Do you see Daddy? Is he here?"

"Well, he will be when I tell him all about you," Linda warned.

"If that gets him here, I'll be surprised, because I've only been trying to get him to come home for the last six months." Clella tossed her purse and coat on the chair by the door.

"That's because he's working," Buck said. Clella nodded. "Yeah, yeah. He's working. And drinking and gambling and probably having more affairs than I ever thought about." Clella looked at Linda and then at Buck. She tried to think of how to explain the relationship between her and their father. "I don't know what happened to Daddy. All of a sudden, he didn't want us around anymore, I guess."

"That's not true," Linda argued. "I'm not listening to this."

"I didn't want to leave Illinois," Clella reasoned. "I wanted us to stay and buy a house. Your dad brought us here and left us out at the farm, not me."

The room was quiet for a moment. Clella felt the lump in her throat. Oh, how she wished she could erase this moment, but she knew that once she had started down that path, that dark slide, sin had wrapped its tentacles around her and pulled her in deeper and deeper. One minute, she believed she had known what was right, but the next, she wasn't sure anymore.

In the beginning, maybe she thought they were just having a little fun. But then, she knew, she had to know, hearts were going to get hurt. She certainly didn't mean to hurt her children.

Sleep didn't come easily for Clella, Linda, and Buck that night. The next morning, there was little conversation except for LouAnn and Larry's bickering at the breakfast table.

Linda called them down. "Why don't you two just eat your breakfast?" Then she turned to Clella. "So, who is he?"

Clella, with skillet in hand, turned and looked at the two younger children before answering. "No one you know," she said quietly.

"Maybe," Buck sat in the chair at the head of table, "But what's his name?"

"I don't think I want to talk about this now." Clella decided not to have any further conversation in front of the smaller children. The smell of bacon and eggs turned her stomach. All of a sudden, she felt very sick. She ran for the bathroom. Her nerves—it had to be her nerves.

A few days passed. Fueled by the stress and tension in her household, Clella woke up each morning sicker than the day before. Linda and Buck weren't talking to her. Of course, she should be sick after all that happened. Just the same, she decided to go see Doc Mott in Hartville.

After her appointment, she drove to a secluded spot by the river. The sky waxed gray and the barren trees of winter mimicked the cold she felt inside. Mud stained all the little patches of remaining snow, making them dirty. She thought about praying, but couldn't. Would God listen to her now anyway? Surely she had stirred His wrath. Besides, she didn't know what to pray. She had always loved Kenneth, but what had happened? Was she so wrong to look for happiness? She knew the answer to that. She should've been stronger. Deceiving her children was wrong, not to mention all the rest of what she had done.

Now she carried another life inside her. Whatever had existed, the love between her and Kenneth, was dead now. Could she ever love him as she did once? She was pretty sure he didn't love her anyway. What about Francis? She didn't know what he would think. He had his whole life ahead of him. He wouldn't want to be weighed down with her. What would he think about the baby? She feared losing Francis the most. She had already lost Kenneth, but to lose Francis might be more than she could bear. She knew there were secret places people went to end pregnancies, but she could never do something like that. Like the woman with the scarlet letter, she would raise this child alone and fatherless.

Chapter Twenty-Seven

Be merciful to me Lord, for I am faint.
......Psalm 6:2

February 25, 1954

Clella nervously fingered the strap of her purse while she waited in the booth at Mag and Ed's tavern. Her stomach turned flip flops. Mag offered her a beer, but she turned it down. She expected Francis anytime now.

Mag sat down beside her sister. "You sure you're all right?" she asked. "You look a little peaked."

"Do I look bad?" Clella asked, suddenly fumbling in her purse for a mirror.

"No, not bad," Mag explained. "Just like you might be a little worried, that's all."

Clella lifted her head and looked directly at her sister. "Oh, Mag, you have no idea."

The door opened and Francis walked in with confident strides, his right elbow jutting out slightly. It was strange, but the moment Clella saw the smile on his face and her eyes connected with his, she felt comforted. This man had brought her happiness when her world had fallen apart. When she was lonely, he was there.

"Hi Mag," he said as Mag vacated the seat for him.

He looked at Clella and for moments their eyes kissed. "Hi, Kid." She laughed nervously. "Is everything okay?" he asked, frowning.

Clella sighed and fidgeted. "I don't know. No, not really. Maybe." She tried not to show that something was different.

He reached out and covered her hand with his. "What is it?" he urged.

"Not here. We have to go someplace where we can talk."

They left the bar and drove out to the west side of town. Just before they reached the saw mill, Francis pulled onto a little grassy spot and parked the car. He turned and kissed her. His lips were sweet as he pulled her closer to him. She knew these might be their last moments of bliss.

When they released each other, he looked at her with concern.

"What is it?" he asked.

Clella nervously looked out the window before facing him again. "The kids know about us. Buck apparently hid in the bed of the pickup when I met you."

He separated himself from her and stared out the windshield. Forever seemed to pass before he spoke. "Well, they had to find out sometime, right? I'm sorry it was like that."

He seemed so calm. Didn't he know how complicated things had become? She twisted the straps of her purse. "There's more, so much more," she said.

"What?" She felt his eyes watching her. He brushed the hair away from her neck and gently massaged it. "Tell me. What's going on?" he asked.

She looked into his blue eyes. She had no way of knowing how he'd react to what she was about to tell him. She had spent sleepless nights trying to figure out what she should do. And there was no way to know until she told him. He shrugged his shoulders impatiently.

"I haven't been feeling well lately. I went to see Doc Mott the other day." She stopped, afraid to continue.

"Yea, what's wrong with you? Are you okay?"

The moment of truth had arrived. She could delay it no longer. She searched his eyes for any indication of how he might react, but the next words she spoke would be life-changing, no matter how he received them.

"Francis, I'm pregnant." She stopped breathing. She watched his eyes change and then bug out.

"You're kidding!" He laughed. Then he grabbed her into his arms. "That's wonderful. Oh, my God. What did the doctor say?"

Clella finally drew a big breath and laughed with the joy of relief. "He said I'm about eight weeks."

Francis placed his hand on her stomach. His eyes brightened like that of a child in a candy store. Clella could hardly comprehend his excitement.

At what point exactly, she thought, *did I end my marriage? Have I?* It was really Kenneth who had decided, wasn't it? She was so confused.

"Well, that settles it for me," Francis said. "I guess I'm going to take that job at Fort Leonard Wood. I'll have to find a house big enough for all the kids." He looked at her and said, "That might be a little difficult."

"What are you talking about?" she asked.

"We're getting married, right?"

"There's this little problem. I'm already married."

"Yeah, but it's over, right?"

"Francis, we can't get married," she announced.

The emotion drained from his face. "What are you saying?"

"I'm saying, I'm forty-one and you're twenty-seven," she reasoned.

"So? You're going to have my baby. That makes things different."

"It isn't going to work. Don't you see? Francis, when I'm sixty you'll be forty-seven." She shook her head. It would just never work. All they had was now. The baby just complicated things in a way she hadn't anticipated.

"So? When you're old, I'll push you around in your wheelchair. What do ya say?"

She laughed for a moment. Then her smile faded. "You don't know what you're saying."

"Do you love me?" he asked.

She smiled. "Oh, Francis, that's one of the problems. I *do* love you!" she answered.

"Well, Kid, I love you. So it's got to work." He traced the outline of her ear with his fingers before kissing her, connecting in an even deeper way.

Clella's heart soared. For a moment, she allowed herself to think of no one but the two of them.

***

Inside the telegraph office, Clella put the pen back in the holder and blew slightly on the piece of yellow paper. Then she read it before giving it to the clerk.

Dear Kenneth (Stop) Urgent you come at once (Stop) Grave news (Stop) (Signed) Clella.

When she handed it to the clerk, tears welled up in her eyes, and a lump formed in her throat. She wanted to run out of there, but unfortunately, she had to tell the clerk where to send the telegram.

Kenneth should receive the telegram sometime this evening. It'll take at least seven hours for him to drive home. She wasn't sure when she would see him, or if he would even come. That's why she added the "grave news", but she no longer knew what motivated him.

***

Kenneth towel dried his hair after showering. When a knock came, Wallace opened the door and received the telegram from the boy. "It's from Mom, Dad," he said. He and Wallace planned to go to Sam's tonight to meet the boys and have a little fun. It was Thursday, but the whole gang would be there. Since they had to work on Saturday, it mattered little whether they went on Thursday night or Friday night.

Kenneth took the telegram from Wallace. Before opening it, he looked at his son. He didn't know why, but he already had a sinking feeling. Something was wrong. He opened it and read it to himself.

"Let's go over to your sister's. I want to call your mother." That was all he said before folding the paper and placing it in his pocket. Audrey had a phone; he and Wallace didn't.

"What is it, Dad? Is something wrong?" Wallace asked.

"I don't know. That's why I need to call."

Audrey later told Kenneth, "The only place I know to call is Aunt Mag's or Aunt Essie's. Then someone would have to go get Mother." Clella didn't have a phone either.

She picked up the phone and dialed her aunt. "Hi, Aunt Essie, Mom wouldn't happen to be there would she?" Audrey held the receiver a little away from her ear. As Kenneth listened intently, he could hear the kids in the background and thought for sure he heard Buck's voice.

"No, Honey, she isn't." Essie's voice sounded different.

"Well, Dad just got a telegram from her saying he should come at once. Is everyone okay?"

"Yes, Honey. You tell him no one is hurt, but that he should come as soon as he can."

"Aunt Essie, what is it? Can Aunt Mag go get Mother and call Daddy back here?"

"No. I don't think that's a good idea. It would be better if he comes himself. Tell him to drive safely, though."

When Audrey hung up the telephone, she looked at her father, puzzled.

Kenneth thought about it. Clella sent a telegram. She didn't go to Mag's or Essie's or somewhere else and call Audrey to get him. At this point, he knew he had to go. He looked at Wallace and then Audrey before speaking.

"I have to leave tonight."

Van started to cry from his crib. "But, Dad," Audrey said, "You'll be driving all night."

Chapter Twenty-Eight

*He who is without sin among you, let him first
cast a stone at her.
......John 8:7 KJV*

Clella did the dishes and scrubbed the kitchen floor.
The house was spotless. Why was that important?
Butterflies danced in her stomach, and the confusion in her
head only grew.

Essie invited the kids to spend the night with her.
Clella had nothing to do now except think about everything.
Her mind floated back to her younger days when she
remembered telling her sister that Kenneth had no
ambition. He wasn't going anywhere. How ironic! He was
the one that had gone and she had been left behind. How
did this happen? How did she let it happen? Surely, she
could've done something. Maybe if she had never met
Francis. What then? She knew the answer. If Kenneth had
his way, she and the kids would be back on the farm with no
running water, and he would be in Illinois doing whatever
he was doing right now.

Kenneth drove all night long. On the way, he
thought about various reasons he might be needed
urgently. Not once did the correct version cross his mind.
He figured there could be some discipline issue with Buck or
Linda, but found it strange that Clella would telegraph in
such a manner for that. Then, he thought maybe Larry was
sick, but Essie would have told Audrey if that was the case.
He couldn't think of anything that Clella couldn't handle
alone. She was always the stronger one and capable of
accomplishing anything. He smiled. He loved that about her.

Deliberately, he had ignored Clella's requests for
him to come home, but he couldn't explain why. He just
didn't want to drive home. He didn't want to see Clella and

the kids. He was so darn mad when he received her letter telling him she rented a house in town. He hadn't even written. He had nothing to say. At dawn, he pulled up outside the house in Mountain Grove. He recognized their pickup parked in the driveway. Beneath the barren trees in the front yard, a remnant of the last snow glittered. A little picket fence outlined the front yard. He looked at the house and softened inside. He imagined it was much like what Clella had searched for in Peoria. The kids would be sleeping, but he could almost see them running out to meet him, shouting over and over, "Daddy, Daddy, you're home!" Guilt fell on him as heavy as an iron curtain. He missed them so much. *And Clella, what would she be doing?* Right now, he imagined her putting on a pot of coffee. He got out and walked slowly to the front door. He stood on the porch for the longest time without knocking.

From the couch where Clella had tried to sleep, she saw him arrive. She waited for him to knock or open the front door. She trembled. How much she wished to avoid what was about to happen. Finally, she turned on the porch light and opened the door.

A little older, but so much the same, he stood on her doorstep, holding his hat in his hand and staring at her with those piercing brown eyes. For one second, she saw him again in the parlor of her parents' house, stumbling over the invitation to teach her how to drive. The first teardrop slipped down her cheek. She opened the screen door and he walked in.

Feelings stirred in Kenneth when he saw Clella. She was his childhood sweetheart, his wife. Even after all these years, how pretty she was. He noticed the tear on her cheek and would have brushed it away with his hand, but the guilt in his heart paralyzed him. He could feel something wasn't right, and, even though his instincts told him he shouldn't, he was still compelled to greet her with a kiss.

She pulled away from him. "Um, I'm glad you came," she said as she turned and walked into the kitchen. "I'll pour you some coffee."

He recognized her reaction. She was angry with him, and with good reason. He took a quick look around before walking to the kitchen and leaning in the doorway. He noticed her hands trembled as she filled their cups. "What's wrong?" he asked. "Where are the kids?"

"They spent the night at Essie and Jim's. They didn't know you're coming. For that matter, I didn't even know if you were coming." She placed the cups of coffee on the table, but neither one sat down. Kenneth looked around the room and then glanced at the round table holding their untouched cups. It wasn't the same kitchen, but it reminded him of the mornings they woke early on the farm. He remembered Daisy bellowing, hungry and needing to be milked, and the rooster crowing at daybreak. He could almost feel Clella's arms encircling him from behind and her lips kissing his cheek. How long ago it all was.

"You told me to come. I came. What's going on?" He approached her, but she crossed to the other side of the room to get the cream out of the icebox. Then she turned and looked directly at him.

"Kenneth," she said softly, "Sit down. We need to talk." After he sat down, she sat across from him. "Kenneth, there are so many things I don't understand. Why did you bring us down here? Why have you stayed away so long?"

"You sent a telegram and I drove all night just so we could talk about this?" he raised his voice slightly in protest. He didn't want to have this conversation. That was why he hadn't come home. That was why he hadn't written. "Clella, I was supposed to be at work today and tomorrow."

For a moment, she just stared at him. Then she sighed. "Kenneth, I want a divorce," she said.

Her words didn't register at first. He couldn't believe what he heard. No one in these parts got divorced.

He took a deep breath. "Clella, you don't mean that. I know you don't mean that. You just want me to come here and live with you the way you want or…"

She interrupted him. "No. I used to want that, but I don't want that anymore."

"I know what you want. You want me to get us a house in Illinois, and we can't afford that."

"Really? We can't afford it? Then how have I been able to do it here? Are you telling me that houses are that much more expensive in Illinois?"

"Actually, they are!" he replied. He placed his cup next to the sink. He couldn't drink any more coffee. His stomach burned like fire. This was the same old Clella: always complaining, always unhappy with something. Either he hadn't dug a well for her, or they couldn't afford to have electricity, or he was drinking and didn't come home soon enough. He could feel that suffocating feeling again, and thought he might faint. He was tired, that was all.

She said it again. Her voice sounded like it came from far away. "Kenneth, I want a divorce."

He needed to sit. He walked into the living room and sat down on the couch.

"You want a divorce? Those cost money."

"Yes, I know."

He looked at her, and for the first time, realized she meant what she said.

"What do you plan on doing? How will you survive with all the kids?"

"They're not just my kids, you know. They're your kids, too."

He stared at her. What was she not saying? "Yes, but why now?"

"What did you expect me to do, Kenneth? Did you not care at all that I was here all by myself, trying to deal with four out-of-control kids?" She pleaded with a hint of anger.

"What are you trying to tell me?"

She stood up and walked to the front window, turning her back to him. "I need a divorce."

"You *need* a divorce?" He watched her with wonder. After several seconds of silence, he dared to ask, "Is there someone else?" He was afraid of the answer. When she remained silent, he stood and walked behind her.

"Yes," she whispered, choking on the word. He turned her around to face him and looked into her tear-filled eyes. He shook his head, but words didn't come.

"Don't look at me like that," she cried. "It's not like we weren't separated. It's not like you wanted me. You had to know I would get lonely. I needed you and you never came." She sobbed.

He could stand it no longer. He reached out and grabbed her, pulling her close to him. From the moment he saw her again, he desired nothing more than to simply hold her. She cried against his chest. He wanted to hold her forever and never let her go.

What had he been thinking? He was lost, but things were clearer now. He ran his fingers through her hair and whispered in her ear, "It's going to be all right. It's going to be all right. We'll figure this out."

Clella felt the comfort of his embrace. How she had longed for it, but too much had changed. She slowly pulled away from him. She wondered if he could see in her eyes the confusion and conflict she felt.

"No, Kenneth. Not this time."

"Yes. Clella, I know I haven't done right, but we can work this out. We'll get the kids and all go back to Illinois."

She couldn't believe what she heard. She turned and walked away from him. "That easy, huh?" *Now* he was willing to live with his family in Illinois.

"I know it won't be easy, but I love you. I've always loved you." She heard his words. They sounded familiar, but they didn't stir the same emotions inside her. She had changed. She could no longer say those words to him. Someone else laid claim to her heart.

"We can't start over and pretend like nothing's happened," she reasoned.

"I know that. I understand." He reached for her, but she pulled away.

She shook her head emphatically. "You don't understand." Tears streamed freely down her cheeks.

"Maybe not, but divorce is not the answer. We're a family. We can work it out."

"Kenneth," she closed her eyes and took a deep breath. "I'm pregnant." She opened her eyes now to see his response. His face had been pale before, but now every ounce of color vanished.

He turned and put distance between them. Minutes passed before he spoke. "Who is he?"

"It doesn't matter. He was there and you weren't."

He glared at her now. "Are you in love with him?"

She glanced at the floor, knowing her response would hurt him even more. "Yes, I am," she admitted.

He sat down and covered his forehead with his hand. "Do the kids know?" he asked.

"Buck and Linda do now." She took a deep breath. "I think they may have told LouAnn and Larry."

"Well, Clella, what do you suppose we do?" he asked. He abruptly stood up and grabbed his hat without looking at her. He headed straight for the door. "I have to go now."

She watched him walk down the sidewalk and get in his car. When he drove away, she sank into the chair and cried.

Chapter Twenty-Nine

Kenneth was definitely sick now. His chest and stomach burned intensely. He drove out of Mountain Grove and over familiar roads toward Hartville. He had to see the kids. All kinds of thoughts ran through his mind. He couldn't believe it came down to this. Perhaps, he deserved what happened. Or perhaps his wife was a harlot! His eyes blurred. He drove erratically and an oncoming farm truck honked at him. He swerved back onto his side of the road.

When he reached Jim and Essie's, the kids ran out of the house. Just as he imagined, LouAnn yelled, "Daddy, Daddy, you're home!" He blinked the blurriness away from his eyes. He hugged all the kids. Buck spoke up next.

"Dad, you need to go talk to Mommy," his son told him.

"Yeah, Daddy, you and Mother need to talk," Linda agreed.

He took a deep breath before telling his children, "I've already seen your mother. I've come to get you. Let's go home."

"Did you know Mommy's got a boyfriend?" little Larry asked.

Kenneth looked above the children to Essie standing in her doorway. He tipped his hat. "Hi, Essie."

"Kenny," she said. "I'm glad you're here." He nodded. "I'm going to take the children home now."

As they drove back to town, Buck told his dad all about that night when he hid in the back of the pickup. Linda added a few details here and there. Kenneth just listened. He didn't really feel like saying anything. He still couldn't believe this was really happening. How great it would be if he could just wake up as if it had all been a nightmare.

When they arrived home, the pickup was gone. Kenneth told the children to stay at home and he would be back. He went to Mag and Ed's tavern.

When he walked inside, Ed was wiping down the bar with a towel. Ed's eyes widened. "Well, hello, Kenny. I didn't know you were in town."

"Just got here today, Ed." Kenneth sat on a stool. He had to find out what his brother-in-law knew.

"So you're not working this weekend, huh?" Ed asked.

This statement perturbed Kenneth. He was beginning to regret staying away all on his own. He didn't need Ed rubbing his face in it! "Ed, let's cut to the chase. What's been going on here?"

Ed leaned across the bar and told Kenneth all about Francis, conveniently leaving out the part where he and Mag introduced the two of them. Kenneth's heart sank. He was a younger man, who played the guitar, and it had apparently been going on for some time. Clella was probably with him right now.

"Can I use your phone, Ed?" Kenneth asked. "Sure. Help yourself."

Kenneth dialed Audrey's number at work. When she answered, he said, "Hi, Sis."

"Dad, is everything all right?"

"You and Alan load up the boys and come down here. Wallace needs to come, too. I have some news. We all need to talk."

That's exactly what happened: Wallace, Audrey, and her family came like Kenneth asked. They all sat down and talked. But just as Humpty Dumpty couldn't be put back together again, it soon became clear that this marriage was broken and no amount of talking could put it back together again.

Audrey found herself alone with her mother in the kitchen. Even though she was grown and had her own family, Clella knew it still hurt her to know her mother and father were getting divorced.

Audrey, who was usually always mild mannered, now raised her voice. "Mother, I don't understand how you could do this to Daddy."

Clella turned to face her. "Audrey, there's so much you don't know."

"I know I would never do what you've done," Audrey lashed out at her.

Clella swallowed hard. "Maybe. Maybe not. As the years pass, marriages go through changes. You don't mean for things to change, but they do."

"I know they don't have to. When you get married, you are committing yourself to your husband forever–in good times and in bad."

Clella sighed. "Your father and I have stuck together through plenty of bad times. That's not it. He just lost interest and now, it's too late." Audrey shook her head and Clella could tell her oldest daughter didn't understand. She was still young and naïve. Clella tried again to reason with her. "You don't know. This could happen to you and Alan one day."

Audrey leaned close to her until their faces were only inches apart. With eyes squinted and narrowed lips, she spewed, "This will NEVER happen to Alan and me." Clella couldn't miss the condemnation. She blinked back the tears. She knew Audrey had reason to be upset with her.

***

One late afternoon in March, Clella loaded the last of her things in the pickup. The kids watched her in disbelief. They hadn't been talking to her. She could only pray that one day, they would all be able to get past this. LouAnn cried. Linda hissed. Buck took out a box that was too heavy for her to lift, his face drawn and forlorn. Little Larry was too young to know what to think.

Clouds threatened rain as Clella backed out of the driveway. The kids finally broke their silence. They ran after the pickup, yelling "Mommy, Mommy!" She should have stopped, but if she had, it would only have prolonged the inevitable.

When she turned the corner on Main Street, tears streamed down her face. Her chest ached, her heart breaking like a fragile piece of china, carelessly slipping through her fingers and falling to the floor. Though, she tried to control herself, she couldn't prevent erupting into shuddering sobs.

She and Kenneth had decided the kids would stay with him. It's what they all wanted. At first, she couldn't imagine leaving her children, but part of her thought Kenneth deserved this honor. After all, she had done her tour of duty.

***

He didn't want to, but Francis finally sat down at his parents' kitchen table. He already felt uncomfortable, and stared out the kitchen window.

"Well, what I'm saying is that you haven't thought this through, Francis," his father, Everette, said. Francis's dad tried to convince him he was making a big mistake. His mother, Anna, refilled their coffees and then sat down next to her husband.

"I don't see that there's anything to think about," Francis replied. "I love her."

"But, she's married and has six children," Anna reasoned. "Why, just last week her daughter, Audrey, came to see us."

"She came here?" Francis raised his brows.

"Yes."

"Why? Was she angry? What did she say?" Francis couldn't believe Audrey came to see his folks.

"She came to tell us you should leave her mother alone."

"She shouldn't have done that." Francis hadn't touched his coffee, but now he picked up his cup and took a drink, wishing he was anywhere else. They would probably never understand, and it didn't matter anyway.

"Francis, let her and her husband try to work things out," Everette said. "It's the right thing to do."

"You don't know what's right," Francis snapped. "You don't know anything about it. Besides, she's getting a divorce."

Anna gasped. "Are you the reason?"

"Maybe," he blurted without thinking. Then he added, "No! Their marriage was over. He doesn't even live here."

"But, she's almost fourteen years older than you," Everette argued.

"That part doesn't matter. I love her." Everette asked,

"What about her children?"

"They've decided to stay with their father." How could he possibly explain to them his love for a woman they had already judged? No matter what he said, they would never understand how she made him feel: intelligent, clever, and capable of doing things of which he had only dreamed.

Francis loved his folks, but his relationship with them had been strained ever since he had left home. Prior to that time, his family of four had attended church out in the country. Music was important to them, and they sang as a gospel quartet. Although Francis loved to play and sing, he didn't feel comfortable doing it in a Christian arena.

Still, his folks could usually coax him into going. He didn't figure, however, that they would ever understand his need for this woman. Perhaps when they met her...

"Francis," Anna spoke, "maybe you should give her some time to think about it and make sure she's doing the right thing."

"That's right." Everette agreed. "Just leave her alone for a time."

"I can't do that."

"Of course you can…"

"Yes, you can. If it's meant to be…" Everette and Anna both spoke at the same time when Francis interrupted them.

"She's having my baby." Silence filled the kitchen.

Chapter Thirty

Kenneth had the weight of the world on his shoulders, or at least it felt like it. He couldn't allow himself to think of his life with Clella as over. Nevertheless, she filed a petition for divorce in Wright County. He started a partnership in an icehouse in Mountain Grove.

Suddenly, he was the one responsible for seeing the kids got to school. It didn't take him long to realize Linda smoked at least a half a pack of cigarettes a day, and Buck liked to hang out with his friends, picking up beer and other alcoholic beverages wherever they could get them. Many times, Linda and her friends could be found in the same company.

March winds continued into April, and the rain showers came as well. One school night, LouAnn finished her homework at the kitchen table. Kenneth noticed she didn't seem her usual self. She was quiet and sullen. She closed her books, laid her pencil down, ran to her room, slammed the door, and fell prostrate on the bed. With her head buried, she cried and cried– loud shuddering sobs that cut him to the core. He didn't know what to do. He walked slowly into her room and sat on the bed next to her. He stroked her hair, trying to soothe her.

"What's wrong, Honey?" he asked. LouAnn rarely exhibited her emotions. "Everything's going to be okay," he assured her, even though he didn't believe it himself.

Whatever he said must have helped. She stopped crying and turned over. With red eyes and a wet face, she looked up at him and asked, "Why doesn't Mommy come home? I wasn't mad at her. Just Linda and Buck were. Get her to come home, Daddy, please? I miss her."

His heart sank. Immediately, he reached out and pulled her into his arms. "I'm so sorry, Honey. I'm so sorry," he said. Why was he apologizing? He guessed he could answer that. He knew he was to blame. All the years he spent following his own desires, the late-night poker games, the ladies with painted lips, and the drinking; it all had taken a toll. He knew that now. How he wished he could do things over again. If he was the only one hurting, it would be more bearable, but when the children suffered, it was more than he could stand. He always thought Clella could handle anything. He never thought she might not be there. How ignorant he had been. He knew now that family was the most important thing in life.

Kenneth tried to pull the kids back into some kind of discipline, but it didn't seem to be happening. He kept busy with the icehouse. The divorce had been finalized two weeks ago. He had held out hope that Clella would change her mind and that they could start again. If he could have convinced her to give it another chance, he would do things differently this time, but, no, she was determined in her decision, perhaps because she was pregnant. But, things could be done these days. She could find a doctor in a secret place that could take care of it. He knew she wouldn't consider that.

Clella moved to Fort Leonard Wood with Francis. He guessed she loved him. He had to plan a future for himself and the kids, but somehow, he didn't really care.

At the end of the day, Kenneth found himself drinking and playing cards, much like in the past. Sleep always came after he passed out from excessive alcohol.

A fine mist-like fog settled over the river. He could hear Clella calling him. "Kenneth," she pleaded, "where are you? Please come home. I miss you." His heart soared as he searched for her in the shadows. "I'm here. I'm coming," he answered. Then he felt her shaking him. He opened his eyes. It was LouAnn.

"Daddy," she yanked his arm, "Come quick. It's Larry. He can't breathe. It's his asthma." Kenneth sat up a little too quickly and the room spun. He ran his hands through his hair and got up. LouAnn led him into Larry's room. Larry's breathing was shallow and his face was pale.

"What do we need to do?" he asked her. Linda and Buck slept soundly. LouAnn went into the kitchen and got Larry's medicine. "This is what Mommy would do," she told him. He did as the instructions said and soon, Larry breathed more easily. With chest congestion and a really bad cough, he wasn't able to attend school at all the next week.

***

Francis tied down the last box in the back of the pickup, checking the tension on the ropes to make sure nothing would fall out during the drive. He got in the driver's seat. Clella sat very still, staring out the window.

"Are you okay?" he asked, clasping her hand in his. She turned to him and smiled through brimming tears. "I'm fine. It's just that not having the kids—it's going to take some getting used to."

"They'll come around. You'll see." He put his arm around her and kissed her. "I hope they do. I'd like it. You know what I mean?" He put the keys in the ignition.

Yes, he probably would, she thought as she watched him. He was so excited about the baby, denying it would be anything other than a boy! If only he was correct about her children, but she couldn't imagine them ever visiting her. They needed to have time with their father right now anyway. It would be good for Kenneth.

Francis put the truck in gear, and together, they drove off toward their new home. He pulled her closer to him and placed his arm around her. Fort Leonard Wood was about seventy-five miles away. Francis was licensed to drive a taxi on and off base. It would pay the bills until he could find something better.

The little cottage was small, but quaint. Each morning, Clella sipped coffee and watched the lilies bloom on the sides of the back porch. Sometimes, she would write Essie or Mag. She wrote Audrey, but guessed her oldest daughter wasn't ready to write back. One day, a letter from Essie arrived. She couldn't wait to open it. There would be news of the children. Her fingers shook as she ripped it open.

Her dear sweet sister declared how much she missed her and had even signed it with, "I love you, your sister." But Clella found the middle of the letter so distressing. "Kenneth was trying," Essie wrote, "but Larry had been awfully sick. Please call Kenny this Friday at 8 p.m. at Mag's tavern." Reading between the lines, Clella could tell that Kenneth still wasn't home much. It fell to Linda and Buck to hold it together. She knew that Linda, Buck, and even LouAnn for that matter, would be okay, but perhaps not Larry. She must do something.

She paced and fretted most of the afternoon, waiting for Francis to get home so she could tell him about Larry. When he arrived, she met him at the door. He hung his hat on the hook, and kissed her.

"You're still up. Are you feeling okay?" Her stomach had started to show and her face had a certain glow.

"I'm fine. I just missed you," she said as she put her arms around his neck.

His arms enfolded her, and he kissed her longer this time. His night hadn't been good. With decreased population on the base, fares and tips weren't what he hoped. When he walked in the door, he felt pretty low, but seeing Clella pregnant with his baby filled his heart with happiness. He slipped his hand beneath her silk gown and caressed her soft skin. "You feel good," he whispered.

"You mean I'm getting fat!" she laughed. "It's a good fat," he said. This time next year, they would have a child. He could hardly contain his excitement. She was the best thing that had happened to him. For the first time in a long time, he had hope for the future. For some reason, he now knew he could pursue his dreams. Somehow, he would overcome a lack of education.

Later, as they snuggled in bed, she told him about the letter.

"I need to call Kenneth and see how Larry is doing."

"But, eight o'clock? That's when I'm the busiest," he protested. "I guess I can take you to the pay phone, but you may have to wait on me while I take a fare or two. We can't afford to lose the money."

They planned for Francis to take her to a little café with a pay phone inside. Sure enough, he got dispatched and had to leave.

Clella opened her coin purse and laid it on the ledge by the phone. She picked up the handset and dialed the operator.

When she answered, Clella said, "Operator, I'd like to call Pershing 8-4511."

"Please deposit twenty five cents for the first three minutes," the operator instructed. Each coin clinked when Clella dropped it into the slot.

The phone rang at the other end. When Mag answered, Clella could hear the jukebox in the background and loud conversation.

"Hi Mag, it's Clella."

"Hang on a minute, he's right here." Mag turned the phone over to Kenneth.

"You there?" he asked instead of the usual greeting.

"I'm here," she answered.

Her voice resonated over the phone in a familiar way, stunning him into a temporary silence. When he was a teenager, he dreamed of her voice. Later, that same voice brought him coffee in the mornings and settled in the evenings on the other side of his bed. How many nights had he missed over the years? He wished he could have them back. He wished he could have her back. He already had a good start on the night's drinking.

"Kenneth?" she asked in the silence. "Yeah?"

"How are things? How are the kids?"

"What do you think?" He heard the animosity in his own tone.

She took a breath, then sighed. "And Larry, how's Larry?"

"He's been pretty sick, but he's doing better now. He needs his mother. They all do."

"You know I would want to take them. They didn't want to go with me."

"School will be out in a couple weeks." He knew better, but he had to try one more time. "Clella, why don't you come back? We can all move to Illinois and start over. We'll be the kind of family..."

"Kenneth," she interrupted him. "Francis and I were married last week." There was a heartbreaking silence over the phone.

"I think Larry should be with you," he finally said.

"Okay. When do you want me to get him?"

"Let him finish school first." He cleared his throat and blinked a few extra times. He realized Mag was listening. He turned away from the bar to prevent being heard. "The last day of school is two weeks from today. I'll take him to school, and you pick him up at the end of the day."

"I can do that. How are the other children?" He took a long drink before he spoke again.

"Oh, you know. They'll be okay. I really got to go." He cleared his throat again. "You take care, now."

"Yeah, you, too," he heard her answer, before he hung up the phone.

Kenneth had Ed pour him another whiskey, which he downed at once, threw some bills on the counter, and walked out.

When he got back home, Larry was there by himself, watching cartoons. Linda and Buck had gone out with friends, and LouAnn spent the night with Catherine Sue. Kenneth tucked Larry into bed. When he thought he was asleep, he walked back into the living room and just stood in the middle of the room.

Finally, he sank to the floor on his knees. He didn't notice Larry, who had heard the thump and climbed out of bed to see what happened. Kenneth beat his fists on the floor, then laid face down on the wooden planks and bawled like a baby.

Larry watched from the doorway of his bedroom, afraid to do anything. He had never seen his father cry before. At seven years of age, he stood helplessly.

Chapter Thirty-One

Clella sat alone, wringing her hands when Francis returned. "How did it go?"

"Kenneth wants me to pick up Larry in two weeks."

His eyes widened. "He does?" he asked. She nodded.

"Well, that may work out pretty well."

"What do you mean?" she asked.

"My brother-in-law just got hired on at Boeing in Wichita, Kansas. I talked to him the other day and he thinks maybe I can get a job there, too."

"Really? Doing what?"

The waitress brought another cup and filled them both with coffee.

"It's an aircraft company. They build planes." He took a sip and continued, "But anyway, I think to leave in about two weeks will work out great. We can go through Mountain Grove and then head west."

Clella listened to him talk. She listened to the excitement in his voice. It all sounded thrilling. If he could get hired, it would be good experience for him and a pretty exciting road trip for her. Still, she couldn't help but think about the tone in Kenneth's voice when she told him she had married. It worried her.

***

It was a beautiful Saturday in May. The birds sang and flew in and out of the cherry trees under clear blue skies. Kenneth took Larry to work with him. Projections for the icehouse that summer seemed more than promising as eating establishments and other events always needed ice.

"Do you want a Grapette?" he asked his son, already knowing his answer.

"Grapette? That's my favorite!" Larry answered. Kenneth smiled and put coins in the soda machine. He opened the top of the machine and slid one of the bottles over to the open slot.

He gave one to his son and then took one for himself. They walked together outside down the sidewalk, stopping on a little bridge. Sitting down there, they sipped their sodas and talked.

"Larry, you know things in life don't always turn out the way you plan. Sometimes you mess up. I mean people mess up."

"Yeah, like I messed up on my spelling test yesterday." Larry smiled, and Kenneth laughed and patted him on the shoulder.

"Yeah, like that. The point is, when people do things that you don't understand, it doesn't mean they don't love you. Many times, they're just trying to find their way. You know what I'm saying?"

"I suppose so," Larry said and took another swig of his soda.

"Son?"

"Yes, Daddy?"

"I want you to always know that I love you." Larry looked up at him with what Kenneth thought might be adoration. Kenneth hugged him.

***

The last day of school finally arrived. Clella parked the green '53 Chevy pickup outside the cafeteria door. The last bell rang, and soon, Larry and his teacher walked out the door. Clella watched his face as he recognized her.

"Mommy," he yelled and started running.

"Hi, Baby," her arms spread wide to receive him. She hugged him tightly. Then she opened the door, so he could see in the middle of the seat a perfect homemade pie.

His eyes bugged out. "Look what I made just for you," she said. "It's your favorite–lemon meringue."

As Clella drove the pickup away from the school, she said, "How would you like to go on a road trip with me?"

"Really?"

"Yep. Francis and I are going to Kansas."

"Francis? And you? And me?"

"What do you say?" she asked. "You want to?"

"Sure. When can I have a piece of pie?"

***

Nothing really mattered to Kenneth anymore. Life no longer held any promise. He tried to find reason to fight or to even exist. He made some decisions over summer, and ironically, he found himself doing the very things Clella had always wanted. He sold the farm, and even though the icehouse had been successful, he wanted to move back to Illinois. So he returned there, rented a house, and got his job back at Caterpillar.

Soon, he and the kids would pack up their belongings and move away from the country where he and Clella had made their start, brought their children into the world, and pursued their own idea of happiness. Thinking about it now, his idea had been quite different than Clella's. Perhaps, he should have been more concerned about other things.

Kenneth pulled into the driveway, put the truck in park, and turned off the ignition. He took a big swig from his flask of whiskey before getting out and going inside to face the kids. It fueled the fire already burning in his chest. He bent over slightly, but got no relief. He straightened back up before Linda, Buck, or LouAnn noticed anything different about him.

"Do you want me to pack these dishes in here, Daddy?" Linda asked.

"That'll be fine, Darling," he replied. He sat down on the couch and tried to catch his breath. Linda, Buck, and LouAnn were excited about moving back. They all worked feverishly to pack and load the truck for the drive to Peoria. They didn't seem to notice he wasn't feeling well, and that was the way he wanted it. It had been a summer of changes. Their mother had left, and she wasn't coming back. He needed them. His decision to move back to Illinois pleased them all.

Late in the afternoon, when they loaded the last box and fitted the last item into the only space left, Kenneth and the kids climbed into the truck and started on their journey. They turned onto Highway 60, and the truck rolled along through the town of Cabool. When they turned onto Highway 63 and headed north, Kenneth had to pull over on the side of the road. Sweat beads rolled down his face, and he walked away from the road slightly, bent over, and vomited.

"Daddy's really sick," Buck said. LouAnn made a funny face and gagged, too, while watching her father.

"I wonder if he's running a fever?" Linda asked, watching anxiously.

Kenneth wiped his mouth with his handkerchief and walked slowly back to the truck. "I'm not feeling too good, kids. Linda, you and Buck are going to have to drive. Linda got behind the wheel and Kenneth sat next to the passenger door.

Linda kept them on course, traveling through Houston, Licking, and toward Rolla. Kenneth coughed every so often.

"Linda, pull over here, now," came his urgent request. She did as her father asked. He threw open the door, and vomited again. This time Linda got out and went to him.

"Daddy, that's red. Is it blood?" she asked as he blotted his mouth with his handkerchief.

"Oh, Honey, no. I drank some tomato juice. That's what it is," he answered. "I'm okay, now. Let's move on."

By this point, all the kids watched their father in silence. He seemed pale, still sweating, and growing weaker by the minute. At Rolla, they took Route 66 toward St. Louis. They were still four and a half hours from their destination. When they reached St. Louis, Linda asked, "Daddy, do you think we should take you to a hospital here?"

"I'll be fine. I'm just a little sick, that's all." Darkness surrounded them about ten miles the other side of St. Louis, when Kenneth needed them to stop again. He barely made it outside the truck. There, standing next to the outside mirror, he vomited again more violently. Linda, LouAnn, and Buck stood beside him.

"Daddy," Linda screamed, "your handkerchief. That's blood. We have to get you some help."

"Honey, we're going home. You can take me to the doctor tomorrow."

Linda glanced at Buck. Buck shrugged. LouAnn drew her face up in distress.

"Buck, help me climb back up into the truck," he ordered. Buck glanced at Linda, giving her a questioning look while helping his Dad. Linda shook her head and shrugged. They didn't know what to do other than what their Daddy told them.

By the time they reached Peoria, the trip had taken three hours longer than usual. Linda and Buck had to help their father walk into the house. In a few short hours, they would take him to the doctor.

Chapter Thirty-Two

There is a way that seems right to a man, but
in the end it leads to death.
......Proverbs 16:25

Audrey, Linda, Buck, and LouAnn all crammed into the exam room. The doctor took one look at Kenneth Lathrom. He directed his order to Audrey. "Take him straight to the hospital, now. I'll meet you there."

Kenneth was so weak he couldn't protest. He wasn't sure why he hadn't wanted them to stop at a hospital the night before. He didn't like doctors and especially not hospitals, but as much as he loved his kids, he just didn't care. Whatever pain he experienced right now, paled next to the thought of going on without Clella.

At the hospital, the staff moved very quickly. Soon, he rested on a bed, drifting in and out of consciousness.

Outside Kenneth's room, Linda shook. "It was blood," she said. "He kept throwing up blood." Audrey listened as her sister retold the story of their trip.

Buck paced back and forth about six feet of space. "He said it was tomato juice. Why would he do that?" he asked.

LouAnn sat on the bench in the hallway. She started crying. Audrey sat down and put her arm around her, but no words came. The doctor walked out in the hallway and motioned for Audrey to join him.

"Your father has lost a lot of blood," he whispered. "We're giving him blood transfusions." He studied her for a moment. "But, I have to tell you, he's critical. All of you can go in and sit with him." Audrey listened through tears she could no longer hold.

"I have to call my older brother. He's at work at Caterpillar."

The doctor put his hand on her back and pointed to the counter down the hall. "The nurses there will dial the number for you," he said and walked her over to the nurses' desk.

With Wallace on his way, the kids all went into their father's room. As the nurses tended him, he threw up bright red blood again. There was precious little the five of them could do. Audrey rubbed her father's forehead. Linda held his hand. Buck sat on the other side of the bed. The tubes carrying life-giving plasma and oxygen were a sight they had never seen. None of them could grasp the gravity of their father's condition.

The doctor talked with Wallace, Audrey, and Linda out in the hall. "He's losing blood at a faster rate than we can replace it."

"What does that mean?" Audrey asked. "What's wrong with him?"

"He's hemorrhaging from a gastrointestinal bleed." The doctor looked to the floor and back up again. He shook his head while explaining, "There's nothing we can do."

Audrey gasped and her knees collapsed at the same time. Wallace, who stood beside her, caught her before she fell.

"Are you saying Dad's dying?" he asked.

The doctor's face said it all. "I'm sorry, Son."

"Oh my God," Linda gasped.

After a moment, Audrey announced, "We should call Mom. I have a number for her in Wichita, Kansas."

"I'm not calling," Wallace said. He dried his eyes with a handkerchief. "I'll be with Dad."

She watched as he walked in and sat at his father's bedside.

Linda looked at Audrey, "I'll go with you. Let's call her," she said.

***

Kenneth opened his eyes just enough to see Wallace and Buck and feel them holding his hands. He tried to gently squeeze them, but he didn't have the strength.

"I love you guys," he managed to say before closing his eyes again.

The room sort of floated. He could hear the birds singing outside. The sun cast a shadowy haze across the room. Out of the shadows, she walked in. She was beautiful, just like he remembered from that day at the river. In fact, she wore the same dress that flowed in the wind. The breeze through the window blew her long brown hair in soft strands around her face. "I'm so sorry," he told her, "for all the things I did." She shook her head and smiled at him while gently caressing his cheek with her hand. She placed a feather soft kiss on his lips. When she rose up, he told her once again, "There's only ever been one girl for me...and I'm looking at her."

"I know," he heard her say as he closed his eyes again and she kissed him on the forehead.

***

Larry was playing ball with the other kids when he heard his name. He threw the ball back to the pitcher. "I guess I've got to go," he told them and ran home. He stopped when he reached the walkway in front of the house. Wayne was waiting for him there on the walk. Wayne was married to Lois, Francis's sister. He usually had a fun, jovial personality, but for some reason, not today. Wayne looked very serious.

"Sit down here on the steps with me, Son," Wayne said softly.

As they sat there on the bottom step, Wayne began. "You know your daddy?"

"Yeah."

"Well, I have something I need to tell you."

"Okay." Larry frowned, wondering what Wayne was going to tell him.

"Your daddy, well..." Wayne took a deep breath and exhaled slowly, "he died today."

Larry knew about death, but at age seven, grasping the complete context was difficult. "Which Daddy?" he asked. "My daddy, Francis, or my daddy?"

Wayne took another long breath, "Your daddy, Kenneth."

Larry sat there for a moment and stared straight ahead. He remembered that day sharing a Grapette with his daddy and their last conversation. For some reason he didn't understand, he started crying and ran inside to find his mommy.

***

The clock on the kitchen wall struck eight o'clock. "I'm worried for her," Francis told Lois. "I don't think it's safe for her to travel right now with the baby only a month away."

"Well, I think it probably is risky, but, Francis, she needs to go," Lois told him. "Larry needs to be there for his father's funeral."

"But think about it," he argued. "It's not going to be easy for her."

"Well, I guess you can try to talk her out of it. I'm not sure that's wise though," Lois said.

He stood up and stared out the window. Only yesterday, everything was fine. In four more weeks, he was going to be a father. Clella had been sewing baby clothes, and just the other day, she had made a baby gown trimmed in pink. "You meant to make that blue didn't you?" he teased.

She laughed and put her arms around his neck. "You aren't going to be too disappointed if it's a girl, are you?"

He smiled, and after a moment said, "You know, I actually think I'd rather the baby be a girl, but we'll see I guess, huh?" She seemed so pleased with his answer. They were going to make great parents. Even Larry seemed excited to have a baby brother or sister. But now, with this awful news, Francis no longer knew what Catherine thought or what tomorrow would bring. If she insisted on going to the funeral, she could deliver the baby too soon.

***

From the dark bedroom, sitting silently on the bed, Clella heard the kitchen clock strike eight. Her hands instinctively went to her belly as the baby kicked. She shed tears earlier, but now she felt numb, not really able to believe it. Since last May, she concentrated on building some kind of new life for Larry, Francis, herself, and their baby. She heard Kenneth was dating a woman, a mother of one of Linda's girlfriends. Essie also wrote her about Kenneth selling the farm and his plans to move with the kids back to Illinois. Never did she think the world would have to exist without him, or that the kids would lose their father. A deep, raw ache racked her body.

She longed to see him once more. She thought about the early days and the dreams she had held so dear. Suddenly, she remembered. She switched on the light and went to the closet. She pulled out a cardboard box, opened it, and took out the picture frame on top. Underneath was a photo book. With care, she lifted it out. She hugged it close to her chest and closed her eyes for a moment. Then she sat back on the bed and slowly opened it.

She smiled. There he stood beside her, holding Wallace in his arms just outside the old grandpa place. He looked so proud. She had been happy then. They had been happy then. She turned the page and found a picture of her, Kenneth, Wallace, and Audrey. A tear slipped down her cheek as she spotted a picture of Kenneth standing beside the old Ford with Linda and LouAnn, who couldn't have been more than three years old. She turned the next page and saw another one in which she and Kenneth sat on the back of their Chrysler. Kenneth had his arm around her, and she remembered the joke he told that had made her laugh. She stared at the images for a long time before closing the book and brushing her hand across the outside. Then she packed it back away in the box and returned it to the same place in the closet.

Chapter Thirty-Three

The one o'clock whistle at the Brown Shoe Factory in Mountain Grove blew louder than Wallace remembered as he stood on the train depot platform, waiting for the 1:10 Burlington Northern from Peoria. The sweltering August heat of 1954 had him dabbing at the drops of sweat on his face and neck with his handkerchief as he stood there alone. It provided the perfect cover for him to also dry his eyes every so often.

As he looked down the railroad track to the east, he saw the dull trees and the occasional car or pickup crossing the tracks. Here in Mountain Grove, life seemed to go on untouched, but in his broken heart, life had come to a horrible stop, suspended in time with little hope for healing. As the train whistle blew, he thought back to the day when he stood on the same platform with his mom, Audrey, and baby Linda waiting for Daddy to come home. Once again, he was waiting for Daddy to come home. The train rounded the curve, and again, the whistle blew. The heat from the engine distorted the air surrounding the locomotive. The train slowed as it neared and finally came to a halt. He dabbed at his eyes again. *This day will surely be the saddest day of my life,* he thought. *Dad won't walk down the steps like he did seventeen years ago.*

Instead, Wallace watched as the men opened the big side door. Minutes later, they carried the coffin down the plank and loaded it into the hearse, which took his father to Barber Funeral Home. The service would be the following afternoon.

***

Clella's heart broke for her children. If only she could somehow comfort them. Even at eight months pregnant, she brought Larry to be with his sisters and brothers. She had decided she wouldn't attend the funeral. Instead, she went early in the morning, when no one else was there. She had to force one foot in front of the other to enter the stately funeral home. After signing the guest book, she started to slowly walk down the aisle and stopped halfway. She wasn't sure she could do this. She flashed back to that schoolroom when they were kids. He had teased her by pulling her pigtails and aggravated her by shooting spit wads. No, she had to do this. She needed to do this. She approached the casket.

How still he lay. There were no highlights in his brown hair, just one or two gray hairs here or there. His fixed mouth didn't curve up on one side into his familiar smile. His eyelids were closed, and she would never look again into his velvet brown eyes. Her hand flew to her mouth as a lump formed in her throat.

She reached out and touched his sleeve. "Why, Kenneth?" she whispered softly. "Why didn't you just love me?" She closed her eyes. In her mind, he stood before her in the middle of the road. He was eighteen and she was sixteen again. "What are you talking about?" she could hear him say as his mouth curved into a smile. "There's only ever been one girl for me, and I'm looking at her."

"I'm so sorry," she told him. She could almost feel him reach out and wipe away the tear on her cheek, could almost hear him saying, "No, Baby, I'm the one who's sorry. We had a good run, didn't we? You take care, now." She nodded and opened her eyes. Turning around, she walked out the door and into the sun.

The funeral was that afternoon. Nothing would be as difficult as that day for the Lathrom children. The Lathrom family had lost a father, a grandfather, and a brother. Many attended—Jim and Essie, Kenneth's brothers, his sister Initia, and Aubrey and Eric. Kenneth was laid to rest with his father at the Robinett Cemetery on Highway 38, just east of Hartville.

Chapter Thirty-Four

*If we confess our sins, He is faithful and just
to forgive us our sins and to cleanse us from
all unrighteousness.
......1 John 1:9*

September 25, 1954

Francis finished the last drop of his coffee, grabbed his lunch box and thermos, and kissed Clella goodbye. He took extra time to check on his wife. "You doing okay, Kid?" he asked, running his hand over the front of her swollen stomach.

She took a deep breath, which seemed harder for her to do these days. "Oh yeah, I'm fine." Her huge belly evidenced that she couldn't go much longer before delivering.

His eyes locked on hers, and he said with all seriousness, "Okay, now, you call that number on the paper. They'll get me and I'll come right away." She nodded. "If you need to go on to the hospital, you call Lois and she'll get you there." Clella nodded and laughed at the same time. "I'm serious," he told her.

"Yes, I know." It was comical and endearing to see how anxious he was for this baby to be born. "You forget I've done this a time or two!" She laughed and started pushing him out the door. "You go on; you're going to be late." He kissed her again.

She watched him walk to the car and drive away to his job at Boeing aircraft. She was proud of him. His superiors had taken little time to recognize his potential, and had offered him on-the-job education and training. He was proving himself worthy of their confidence.

Larry soon left for school. Clella sat alone, finishing her cup of coffee. Her bittersweet life held in one hand hope and a future, and in the other, sadness and regret. So much had changed in such a short time. Wichita was a good place to live. Although she was excited to be in a new place, she missed home, her sister, and her children. Sometimes, she felt as if a dagger pierced her heart.

She noticed a Bible on the coffee table. It belonged to Lois. She opened it and randomly turned toward the back cover. She stopped at the first chapter of First John. As she read, verse nine caught her attention. "If we confess our sins," she read, "He is faithful and just to forgive us our sins." The words seemed to jump off the page and were almost more than she could comprehend. She freely accepted the personal guilt which weighed so heavily.

"God," she prayed. "You indeed are merciful." Tears rolled freely down her face. "Please forgive me," she pleaded. She knew in that instant God had forgiven her, but could she ever forgive herself? Perhaps, she had no right to feel any happiness.

Later that morning, Clella finished the dishes and picked up the living room. When she leaned over to make the bed, her water broke. This was it. Her seventh child was about to enter the world. She called Lois, who said she would be right there. She called the number Francis had given her.

Soon, orderlies wheeled her through the hallway of St. Francis Hospital, taking her to labor and delivery. By the time Francis arrived, she was progressing rather quickly. He paced in the waiting room.

"Push, Clella," the doctor instructed. "Push."

Will my baby be healthy? Clella worried as she pushed.

"I see the head. Push again, Clella." She bore down and gasped.

Finally, "It's a girl, Clella. You have a perfect little girl," she heard the doctor's voice above faint crying.

She couldn't help but think about her other children. How were they doing after the loss of their father? Her heart ached, knowing they had been divided up among relatives, like orphaned children being torn apart and placed in foster care. At least they went to homes of loved ones. Linda went to live with Audrey. Buck traveled with Uncle Aubrey to Washington State. Aunt Initia wanted LouAnn to live with her. She had no children of her own, and spoiling LouAnn was right up her alley. But oh, how Clella missed her children.

She soon held her precious bundle in her arms. Francis hovered over them. His face beamed and he acted giddy. She smiled as she watched him. As they decided on a name, the baby wrapped her little fingers around one of Clella's. It had been almost eight years since she had had a newborn. Tears threatened as Clella knew she had to love and protect this new little life God had given her, but she needed her other children. She needed to know they were okay.

"What's wrong?" Francis asked.

"Where's Larry?"

"He's with Wayne and Lois," he answered. "The hospital won't let him come in here."

"I know. I just wish all the kids were here and they could see their new baby sister."

"They'll eventually come around. You'll see," Francis told her as he took the baby from her arms. She wasn't so sure and it tormented her.

***

Once home, Francis couldn't be more proud as he watched his wife with his baby girl, Diane. Sitting in an oversized chair, he held out his arms and took the infant from her. Clella sat on the side of the chair and put her arm around him. Larry knelt close by, all posing for a photograph. Just before the flash and the snap of the picture, Larry looked up at his baby sister.

The next year proved Francis's prediction about Clella's children right. First, Convair in Texas offered Francis a job. He, Clella, Larry, and the baby moved to Fort Worth not far from Carswell Air Force Base. It was much hotter in Texas than they were used to, but they rented a house on the lake. Francis continued to develop skills in aerospace that would serve him well, and just as he said, her children eventually came around.

Buck and LouAnn soon joined their mother, little brother, and new baby sister. Even Linda, now straight out of high school, hired on at Convair and moved nearby.

In 1955, amidst the emergence of rock 'n' roll and aerospace, the four younger Lathrom children liked living with their mother again and warmed to the idea of her being married to Francis.

Buck and Larry both loved to play the harmonica and go fishing. Some evenings and weekends, they fished together with Francis at Lake Worth. Other times, they all played music together, like "The Orange Blossom Special" and the "Wabash Cannonball". Francis played the guitar, and Buck and Larry played lead on their harmonicas. Linda and LouAnn sang with them and danced.

One mild autumn evening, Clella sat outside on the back porch and looked out over the water. Sunlight flickered over the ripples, providing a soothing effect. She thought about Missouri and the farm. She missed Essie. Then she heard Buck and Larry fishing with Francis off the dock below. It sounded like they must have caught a big one and she would soon be frying catfish. She smiled.

Kenneth would always hold a special place in her heart, and she would probably always ache whenever she remembered him, but if God allowed Kenneth to look down from above, then perhaps he could rejoice that his children were all together again.

***

Clella's story reminds us that no one is perfect. Clella wasn't perfect. Kenneth wasn't perfect. There is only one who was and is perfect. He is our Lord and Savior Jesus Christ. Yes, I said "our" because He died for all of us who will believe. Clella's story didn't end here. For me, it had just begun. But, when it was over, her children rose up and called her "*blessed*".

The End

For we know that all things work together for good, for those who love God who are called according to His purpose.
......Romans 8:28 KJV

Larry, Clella, Diane, and Francis, 1954

Afterword

I thank God who gave me the courage and opportunity to share the story of my mother and our family. It is a story of redemption, but then, after all, when one calls upon the Lord, there is always redemption. Man, who was made with a free will, often walks away from God, yet when he repents, God always hears and rescues him from evil.

I first met my Savior when I was eleven. My dad, mom, and I lived on a farm about seventy miles west of St. Louis. One night, I looked outside the window next to my bed. I remember the beautiful night and the stars that shined brighter than usual. The whole sky glowed with, what I realize now was, the glory of God, because he was knocking at the door of my heart. In that instant, I knew I was a sinner and desperately needed to repent. Right then, I prayed. I didn't worry if I said the right words or if I bowed my head a certain way. I just asked God to forgive me and He did. I believe my experience was much the same as Isaiah in Isaiah Chapter 6. He saw the Lord *"high and lifted up,"* and suddenly he said, *"Woe is me...for I am a man of unclean lips."*

Only God, through the blood of Jesus Christ, can cleanse our hearts and change our unyielding lives. He knew us before we were born and He is not willing that any should perish, but that all should come to repentance.

Just like my mother, I often forget that the one who created me is *"an ever-present help in trouble,"* and many times, I try to fix things on my own. I am learning daily to rely more and more on Him. Wherever you are now in the journey of your life, God is always there, always ready to hear you when you call. He truly cares about you and not only will he *"supply all your needs"*, but he also wants to *"give you the desires of your heart."*

May God richly bless you and your family,
.....*Diane Yates*

Garner Family approx. 1922

Clella and Daisy 1929

Clella age 16, 1929

Clella, Wallace and Kenneth 1931

Kenneth plowing with Audrey approximately 1935

Kenneth, Audrey, Wallace, Clella 1933

Wallace, Linda, Buck and Audrey 1943

Bath time for Wallace and Audrey 1933

Playtime for Wallace and Audrey 1934

Audrey, Buck, Clella, Linda, Wallace, and Kenneth, 1943

Audrey, Buck, LouAnn, and Linda 1946

The swimming hole with Clella and the kids,
approx. 1947

Audrey and Hettie Pauline in feed sack dresses, 1948

Audrey wearing the jumper Clella made, 1949

Larry, LouAnn, Buck, and Linda, 1952

Larry and LouAnn, 1953

LouAnn, 1953

Aunt Essie, Hattie Pauline, James G. and Uncle Jim
Year unknown

Made in the USA
Lexington, KY
25 September 2017